Right into Reading

A Phonics-Based
Reading and
Comprehension
Program

Jane Ervin

Book
2

Educators Publishing Service
Cambridge and Toronto

About the Author

Jane Ervin works in Washington, D.C., with children with reading and learning differences, and advises parents on educational concerns. Dr. Ervin has written more than 20 books for students, teachers, and parents; her workbooks have sold over 5 million copies. She received her Ed.D. and postdoctoral diploma from UCLA.

Acknowledgements

I would like to thank the National Geographic Society for their interest in the development of these books, and particularly the editors of *World* magazine, whose lively, interesting articles provided a stimulating resource that contributed greatly to the quality of the readings. I would also like to thank the numerous teachers and students with whom I have worked for their encouragement and suggestions during the development of this program. Special thanks to Jo Ann Dyer, who has been involved in so many of my projects, for her errorless manuscripts as well as her enthusiastic support. Thanks also to the production team: Wendy Drexler for her editorial work and painstaking attention to detail; Tatjana Mai-Wyss for her appealing illustrations; and Joyce Weston for her assistance in the cover design and layout of the workbook.

Printed in U.S.A.
ISBN 0-8388-2603-2
September 2002 Printing

CONTENTS

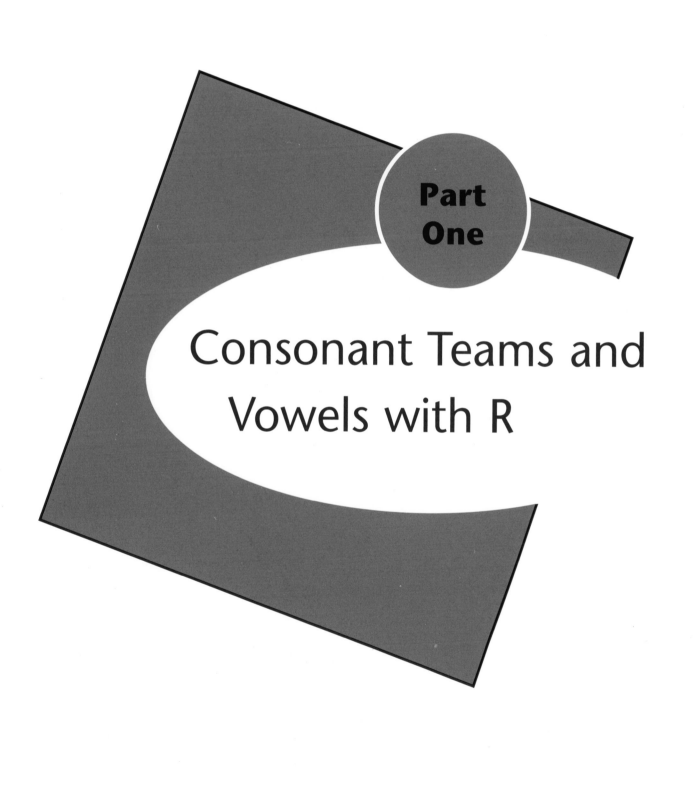

Part One

Consonant Teams and Vowels with R

When **S** and **H** come together,
they have **one sound.**

shop

fish

Sound out the letters to read each word.

shut	ship	shade	shell
dish	sheet	shine	show
wish	shake	cash	shed
rush	rash	shot	shall

shape	crush	shock	crash
brush	shelf	flash	trash
shave	finish	shallow	fresh
shadow	vanish	selfish	polish

Learn to read these words: should would could
These words have the **sh** sound: sugar sure

→ Choose a word from the list above to answer each riddle.
Write the word on the line.

1. A tree will give you this on a hot day: _____

2. You use it to paint: _____

3. It's the opposite of open: _____

4. The sun does this: _____

5. It is used on a bed: _____

6. To end something: _____

→ Circle the name of the picture.

	shall		rush
	shell		crush
	shelf		blush
	self		brush
	flush		shade
	flash		shall
	flesh		shallow
	fish		shadow
	shin		snake
	shrink		shake
	show		shack
	shot		stack
	cash		shave
	rash		shade
	trash		slash
	track		splash

→ Choose a word from the list to complete each sentence. Write the word on the line.

1. "Say, Dan, will you give me a hand _____ the truck?" asked Shamel.

2. "Are you _____ that you don't need any sugar in your coffee?" asked Sharlene.

3. "It's safe to swim," said Shaka. "The lake is _____."

4. Kayla told Brad that he was _____ when he would not lend her his bike.

5. "These cupcakes are great!" exclaimed Josh, _____ the last one.

6. The baseball score _____ across the TV screen: Cubs, 4; Mets, 3.

finishing

polishing

shallow

flashed

selfish

sure

➔ Draw a line to the correct ending of each sentence. Then put an X in the box next to the sentence that tells about the picture.

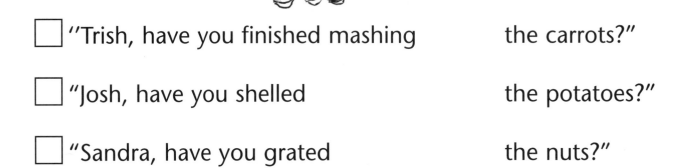

☐ "Trish, have you finished mashing   the carrots?"

☐ "Josh, have you shelled   the potatoes?"

☐ "Sandra, have you grated   the nuts?"

☐ "Dick has a rash so I am taking him to   the mailbox?"

☐ "Jeff, will you rush this note to   the trash can?"

☐ "Kim, will you take this rubbish to   Dr. Sharks."

- [ ] The oak tree cast a shadow   behind him.

- [ ] Lee could see his shadow   on the plants.

- [ ] Jean vanished into the shadows   to hide.

- [ ] Dad pulled up the sheets on   the window.

- [ ] Mom pulled up the shades on   the dishes.

- [ ] Grandma finished doing   the bed.

Can You Make a Solid Vanish?

📖 Read the passage.

See if you can tell what the words **vanish** and **dissolve** mean.

Learn to read these words: **water warm**

You can see and feel a solid. But can you make it vanish?

Take sugar. It is a solid that you can see and feel. Can you make sugar vanish? Yes.

One way to make sugar vanish is to put it into **warm water**. Fill a glass with **warm water** and add sugar to it. You will see that it disappears in an instant.

Is the sugar still there? Take a sip. Does it taste sweet? Yes, it does, so the sugar is still there.

The reason the sugar vanishes is that sugar dissolves in **water**. It breaks up into bits of sugar, named molecules (mol-e-cules). These molecules mix with the **water**.

→ Circle the correct answer.

1. Vanish means   (a) appear   (b) disappear

2. Dissolve means   (a) break up   (b) become a solid

3. You can make sugar vanish if you
      (a) crush it   (b) shake it   (c) put it into water

4. The water you put the sugar in tastes sweet.
      (a) yes   (b) no

5. Is the sugar still in the water?   (a) yes   (b) no

6. The sugar bits that the sugar breaks into are named
   molecules.   (a) yes   (b) no

Can you get the solid sugar back? Read on!

Yes, you can get the solid sugar back.

Put the sugared **water** into a shallow pie dish. Leave the dish in a **warm** spot. In time the **water** will vanish and the sugar will be left in the dish.

Do you end up with the same sugar that you began with? Yes. No sugar is lost as it dissolves.

➜ Circle the correct answer.

1. You get the solid sugar back by
   (a) straining the water   (b) shaking the water
   (c) putting the water in a shallow dish

2. You put the dish in a warm spot.   (a) yes   (b) no

3. Some of the sugar is lost.   (a) yes   (b) no

4. Sugar is a solid.   (a) yes   (b) no

5. Sugar can become a liquid.   (a) yes   (b) no

✎ Write at least 3 sentences describing something made from sugar, such as candy or brownies.

When **CH** come together,
they have **one sound.**

cheese

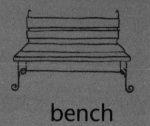

bench

Sound out the letters to read each word.

chin	chop	chain	such
cheek	rich	chase	much
cheese	teach	lunch	cheap
peach	check	chest	branch

pinch	chip	inch	French
Chuck	punch	chill	coach
cheat	munch	cheer	chopsticks
chicken	chipmunk	sandwich	children

If there is a **t** before the **ch**, it is not sounded.

ca~~t~~ch   i~~t~~ch   hu~~t~~ch   sco~~t~~ch   fe~~t~~ch

Learn to read these words that have the **long i** sound:
child   mild   wild

➔ Draw a line between the words that rhyme.

beach	much	chin	shin	bench	French
such	mild	chip	ship	itch	wild
child	peach	chop	shop	mild	witch
chest	vest	chill	Dutch	cheap	teach
cheer	match	choke	broke	rich	heap
catch	dear	clutch	frill	each	hitch

→ Add **ch** to find the name of each picture. Then write the number of the picture in the box.

☐ wat_____

☐ _____ina

☐ pea_____

☐ _____ipmunk

☐ in_____

☐ _____icken

☐ mat_____es

☐ _____opsticks

☐ stit_____

1.

2.

3.

4.

5.

6.

7.

8.

9.

➔ Read each sentence and circle the missing word.

1. Chelsea munched on her lunch of _____ sandwiches.
    (a) chocolate (b) peach (c) chicken

2. Mom chose a cheese dish and Dad had a pork _____.
    (a) chunk (b) chip (c) chop

3. Chip stitched a _____ onto his jeans.
    (a) pinch (b) pitch (c) patch

4. "It's difficult to eat a _____ pie
    with chopsticks!" said Chad.
    (a) each (b) peach
    (c) beach

5. The French, _____, and English came to America in the
    1600s.
    (a) witch (b) clutch (c) Dutch

6. Shay ran fast to _____ the baseball in his mitt.
    (a) match (b) catch (c) fetch

➜ Chuck is in the kitchen fixing his lunch to take to school. Put an X next to the sentence that tells what you think Chuck will do to make his lunch. Then **see** how many **ch** words you can find.

☐ Chop up a tomato

☐ Make a chicken sandwich

☐ Add a pinch of sugar to his sandwich

☐ Cut cheese into chunks

☐ Add 2 bags of chips

☐ Take two peaches to put into his lunch pail

☐ Munch on a rich, chocolate cupcake

☐ Make a bowl of chili

☐ Pack a drink of chilled punch

How many **ch** words did you find? _____

Cheena Has Lunch

📖 Read the story.

"I'll have to get lunch. It's past one o'clock and I'm hungry," said Cheena.

She went into the kitchen and had some chicken. But that did not fill her. So she fixed herself a cheese sandwich. She ate the sandwich, but that did not fill her. Next, she had a chocolate cupcake. But she was still not full.

"Oh dear, I seem to have eaten a lot. There is not much left," she said to herself. "Let's see, there's a peach. I'll eat that."

She ate the peach and, at last, she was full.

"That was so stupid," she said. "Why didn't I eat the peach to begin with? Then I would still have the chicken, the sandwich, and the cake left!"

→ Circle the correct answer.

1. Why did the peach make Cheena full?
   (a) it was a big peach
   (b) she had eaten a lot by the time she ate the peach

2. Cheena did not eat
   (a) chicken   (b) chips   (c) a cheese sandwich

3. If she had eaten just the peach would Cheena have been full?   (a) yes   (b) no

4. Put these in the order that Cheena ate them:
   _____ cheese sandwich
   _____ chocolate cupcake
   _____ chicken

✎ Cheena had a lot to eat. Write about some of your favorite foods.

3

three

When **TH** come together,
they have **one sound.**

teeth

Sound out the letters to read each word.

this	teeth	with	think
cloth	that	thank	throw
sixth	bath	three	moth
throne	thin	thrown	thud

breathe	thump	thing	fifth
path	theft	thrill	thankful
math	throat	thumb	seventh
depth	width	length	Thanksgiving

Learn to read these words:
 something   nothing   anything   month   mother
In these words the **s** has the **z** sound: these   those

→ Choose a word from the list above to answer each riddle.
Write the word on the line.

1. It's an American holiday: _____

2. Your lungs help you do this: _____

3. It comes after fifth: _____

4. The opposite of thick is: _____

5. You use it to swallow: _____

➔ Add **th** to find the name of the picture. Then write the number of the picture in the box.

☐ wid_____

☐ no_____ing

☐ ba_____

☐ mon_____

☐ _____roat

☐ pa_____

☐ leng_____

☐ mo_____

1.

2.

3.

4.

5.

6.

7.

8.

➔ Read the sentence and circle the missing word. Then write the word on the line.

1. "Would you help me with this _____,
   please?" asked Ezra.

   bath   path   math

2. Brad is going into the _____ grade.

   fifth   filth   froth

3. "I don't want _____ to eat, thank you,"
   said Beth.

   something   nothing   anything

4. "I'd like ten of those cupcakes and seven of
   _____ sweet buns, please," said Mr.
   Nemeth.

   them   this   these

5. "I _____ that I will be an
   actress when I grow up," said Thelma.

   thin   think   thank

➔ Put an X next to the correct answer.

Which one would be the **thickest**?

_____ (a) the tail of a chipmunk

_____ (b) something made from cloth

_____ (c) the branch of an oak tree that is three feet wide

Which one would be the **thinnest**?

_____ (a) the wing of a moth

_____ (b) the throat of a man

_____ (c) the teeth of a child

Which one would have the greatest **width**?

_____ (a) a freeway that has 4 lanes

_____ (b) a box the size of a matchbox

_____ (c) a cloth as big as a bed sheet

Which month was the **wettest**?

_____ (a) in April there was some snow

_____ (b) in May there were brisk

winds and many days of rain

_____ (c) in June there were many

days filled with sunshine

The Three Wishes

As you read this story, try to read several words at a time instead of word by word.

A long time ago, a man named Seth lived with his wife, Ethel, in a thatched home near a forest. Each day he went into the forest to cut trees and chop them into logs.

One day, as he was chopping, he said to himself, "Oh dear, I'm so upset. I don't own much and I don't get paid much. Oh dear, life is so difficult."

The moment he finished there was a flash. Much to Seth's astonishment, an elf jumped from the branch of a beech tree and landed on the path next to him.

"I hope I didn't shock you," exclaimed the elf, grinning. He was thin and just three inches in size. He had wings like a moth's, deep black eyes, an unshaven chin (yes, a beard!), and cheeks as red as his red cloth cap.

"N-no! N-no, you d-did n-not," replied Seth. But he was shaking from the shock. Then the elf cleared his throat, puffed up his chest, and said, "Dear man, I think I can help you."

"Th-thanks, th-thanks a lot," said Seth.

"I am going to grant you three wishes— any three wishes you wish to make!" said the elf.

"Oh, thank you, thank you!" exclaimed Seth. He was thrilled. But by then, the elf had vanished into the shadows of the trees.

→ Checking up: See if you have followed the story. Circle the correct answer.

1. Seth is not rich.   (a) yes   (b) no

2. Seth has a difficult life.   (a) yes   (b) no

3. An elf came from a tree.   (a) yes   (b) no

4. The elf was 6 inches in size.   (a) yes   (b) no

5. The elf gave Seth one wish.   (a) yes   (b) no

Seth rushed home to tell his wife, pinching himself all the way to make sure he was not dreaming!

He got home to find Ethel cleaning and polishing. He had taken his lunch to the forest, so she was not expecting him.

"Oh dear, I hope you're not sick!" she cried.

"No, I'm not sick," Seth exclaimed, smiling.

Then he said, "An amazing thing happened in the forest.

I met an elf and he said that I could have any three wishes that I wish. Isn't that great? We can be rich at last!" he added!

"Yes, I am so happy," said Ethel.

Then she said, "Let's have lunch and think of the wishes we want to make."

Seth got his lunch pail and Ethel fixed herself a sandwich.

"We'll have a big home," said Seth.

"Yes. Then we can have a lot of children. I'd like a lot of children," said Ethel.

"Me, too," said Seth. "And we'll get some fine clothes, so you can dress like a queen," said Seth.

"And you can get that plot of land you have always wanted," said Ethel.

"Yes," agreed Seth.

He had a bite of stale cheese, still thinking of the things he was going to have. Then he said, "This cheese is like a rock. I wish I had a big, fat hot dog."

In a flash, a big, fat hot dog was on his plate! Seth and Ethel were amazed.

"Oh, no!" exclaimed Ethel. "You have used up one of the wishes."

"Yes, that was a mistake," replied Seth, "but I still have two wishes left. We can still be rich and have the things we want."

"But not as rich as if we still had the three wishes," complained Ethel.

She went on complaining until, at last, Seth said, "Oh, hush! I'm tired of your complaining. I wish that hot dog was hanging from the end of your nose!"

In a second, the hot dog was on the end of Ethel's nose!

"Oh Seth, you did it again!" she screamed, shaking her nose to get the hot dog off.

"Yes, I was not thinking," agreed Seth. "But we can still be rich. We have a wish left."

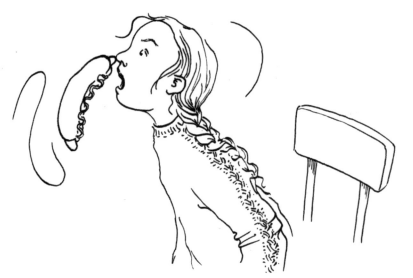

Ethel was so mad. "You can think of nothing but getting rich. You must help me get this THING OFF!" she screamed.

→ Checking up: See if you are still following the story. Circle the correct answer.

1. Ethel was reading at home.   (a) yes   (b) no

2. Did Ethel think Seth was sick?   (a) yes   (b) no

3. Ethel hugged Seth.   (a) yes   (b) no

4. Seth ate a hot dog.   (a) yes   (b) no

5. The hot dog ended up on Ethel's nose.   (a) yes   (b) no

Ethel began to shake the hot dog again, and went on shaking it until her cheeks were red.

"I'm so mad at you, the wishes, and—and—your hot dog!" she screamed. The hot dog swayed from side to side, and Ethel began to cry.

"Oh, I wish that hot dog would go away!" cried Seth.

In an instant the hot dog vanished. Ethel's nose was just as it had been. And so were the lives of Ethel and Seth. They had been given three wishes by the elf, but they still had no big home, no riches, and no children. And they did not even have the hot dog, so they still had to eat the stale cheese!

→ Now reread the story and circle the correct answer.

1. The main idea of the story is
    (a) Seth met an elf
    (b) Ethel got a hot dog on her nose
    (c) Seth wasted his three wishes

2. Seth   (a) was sick   (b) did not think

3. The wishes made Seth and Ethel
    (a) happy   (b) unhappy

4. Was Seth's last wish a wise one?   (a) yes   (b) no

✎ If you were given 3 wishes, what would you wish for?

wheel

When **WH** come together, they have **one sound**.

whale

Sound out the letters to read each word.

while	white	when	which
wham	wheat	whine	whack
whip	whale	wheeze	whiff

whisk	whiten	wheel	whiz
whipping	whereas	meanwhile	wheelbarrow

Learn to read these question words:

who   whom   whose   where   why   what
whole

→ Read the sentences to understand the meaning of the words in bold print.

1. Jack finished packing **while** Anna loaded the van.
2. "**Who** is going on the trip?" asked Ethan.
3. "Will you cut up the **whole** melon, please?" asked Rachel.
4. The **whiff** of Vadim's baking made them hungry.
5. Dad said, "**Whip** up the cream and then **whisk** the egg whites."
6. **Whales** are the biggest animals in the sea.
7. Chip's dog Spot **whined** to come inside.
8. "Do you want jam or cheese on your whole-**wheat** toast?" asked Brandon.

➜ Now match the words with their meanings.

_____ 1. who   (a) at what time

_____ 2. whole   (b) which one

_____ 3. when   (c) total

_____ 1. whale   (a) a sea mammal

_____ 2. whine   (b) complain, moan

_____ 3. while   (c) at the same time as

_____ 1. wheat   (a) to beat; to go fast

_____ 2. whisk   (b) a grain

_____ 3. white   (c) a color

_____ 1. whip   (a) it helps things move

_____ 2. wheel   (b) to beat, lash

_____ 3. whiff   (c) a puff, wave of a smell

→ Choose a word from the lists on page 28 to complete each sentence. Then write the word on the line.

1. "_____ is coming home with me?" asked Kaylee.

2. "I'll be there in a _____," said Emil.

3. It's best to _____ the eggs if you're scrambling them.

4. Jonathan's bike needs a new _____.

5. "_____ will we get there?" asked the children.

6. "Are you going to eat the _____ pizza?" Jenna asked in amazement.

7. The President's home is painted _____.

8. The _____s swim up the coast to Alaska when the water gets warm.

→ Write the name of the question word next to its meaning. Then write the question word in the sentence.

who   **when**   **which**

1. What person: _____
   "_____ helped you?" asked Ms. White.

2. What one, or ones: _____
   "_____ one do you like best?" she asked.

3. At what time: _____
   "_____ do you get home from school?" asked Grandma.

why   **what**

4. For what reason: _____
   "_____ did you do that?" asked Mom.

5. Which thing: _____
   "_____ is your name?" asked Mr. Whitcliff.

whose   **where**

6. In, or at, what place: _____
   "_____ is your school?" asked Grandpa.

7. The one, or ones, belonging to someone: _____
   "_____ are these socks?" asked Dad.

Wanda the Whale

Read the story and write the correct question word on the line where a word is missing. Then reread the story to see if it makes sense.

Use these question words:
who what when where which why

Learn to read these words: **beautiful very tiny air**

Learn the meaning of this word: **expel**

Wanda the Whale is said to be the biggest blue whale living in the waters off the coast of Mexico. She is a blue whale,

_____ is the biggest animal living today. This means that Wanda is **very** big. In fact, she is 90 feet long!

_____ she was a baby she was as big as an elephant (el-e-fant).

Who would have said that Wanda would grow up to be so **beautiful**? And she is **beautiful,** too. You can see this as she jumps from the water. This is called breaching.

Wanda seems to be smiling as she leaves the water. She has no teeth, unlike the orca whale. No, like many whales,

she has 2 rows of plates called
baleen, _____
grow in long strips.

_____ Wanda takes
in water, the baleen catches lots
of **tiny** sea creatures that
Wanda likes to eat.

_____ Wanda
expels the water, the creatures
get trapped in the baleen plates.

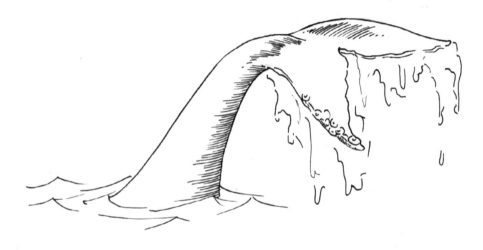

Wanda has a handsome tail, too. She swishes it from side
to side in the water,
using her flukes.

_____
are flukes? They are
the two wings at
the end of a whale's
tail.

→ Checking up: see if you have followed the story.

1. Wanda is big. (a) yes (b) no

2. Wanda is a white whale. (a) yes (b) no

3. "Breaching" means breathing. (a) yes (b) no

4. Whales have no teeth. (a) yes (b) no

5. Wanda uses baleen to swish her tail. (a) yes (b) no

6. Wanda feeds on big fish. (a) yes (b) no

Wanda is known for the big spray from her blowhole, _____ goes up, up, up for 20 feet! That is a long way! The blowhole is the hole on top of a whale's head (hed) that lets **air** into its lungs. _____ a whale dives, it keeps in the **air** and stops breathing. _____ it comes up again it **expels** the **air** in a big spray of water.

Wanda has a baby named Wham, _____ will be one year in a week. Wanda is planning to leave the warm Mexican waters _____ they have been during the winter months. She and Wham will swim up the coast to the chilled waters of the Arctic. _____ do you think they do this? They will swim up the coast to eat lots of those **tiny** sea animals that they like so much.

➔Circle the correct answer.

1. Whales use blowholes to   (a) eat   (b) breathe

2. Wanda's spray goes up   (a) 12 feet   (b) 20 feet

3. A whale stops breathing when
     (a) it is in the water
     (b) it is breaching

4. In one week, Wham will be   (a) one month   (b) one year

5. The Mexican waters are   (a) warm   (b) chilled

6. Wanda is taking Wham up to the coast to the Arctic
     (a) to have fun
     (b) so they can still eat the tiny sea animals

✎ Write more about Wanda and Wham. You can make up a story about them. Or you can find out more facts about blue whales.

LESSON 4: CONSONANT TEAM WH

Read the words and circle the consonant teams.

sh ch th wh

thing	white	chin	show
whale	cloth	which	chest
wheat	length	three	lunch
chicken	wheel	shadow	math
fetch	itch	selfish	width
shelf	whereas	Chinese	breathing

➜ Read the sentence and circle the missing consonant team. Write the missing letters on the line.

1. Josh _____inks he can catch ten fish.   sh   ch   th

2. The chipmunk mun_____ed on a nut.   wh   th   ch

3. The back _____eel on Chip's bike is broken.   th   ch   wh

4. Dad likes to eat _____ellfish when he can get them.   sh   ch   th

5. The smell of the fre_____ whole-wheat loaf whetted Nick's appetite.   ch   th   sh

6. "_____o put all that sand in the wheelbarrow?" asked Jade.   th   wh   sh

7. "Whi _____ clothes do you want me to wash?" asked Kevin.   sh   ch   wh

8. There are twelve mon_____s in a year.   ch   sh   th

→ Circle the name of the picture.

a shallow dish
a punch bowl

a thick cloth
a thin shell

a wheelbarrow of branches
a shelf of china

a crushed peach
a fresh fish

a crying child
a chuckling chicken

a tree in the shade
a ship at sea

throwing a ball
washing clothes

finishing a fish
cutting up a pork chop

➜ Read these fun sentences. Then see how fast you can say them.

1. Are you sure six selfish shellfish should shave?

2. Chuck chatted as he chopped chunks of chilled chicken.

3. Why won't Wilma the wicked witch wait for the white whale?

➜ **What Am I?**

I grow on a tree. I am yellowish pink and have a skin. I taste sweet and I am best to eat when I am fresh. I have a stone inside me. I am not as big as a melon, but I am not as small as a plum. I end with a consonant team.

I am a _____.

➜ Put an X on the line next to the sentence that answers the question.

1. **Why** does a snake shed its skin?

___ (a) A snake's skin is made of scales.

___ (b) The snake's skin is thick and can shine.

___ (c) As a snake grows, it gets too big for its skin. The skin splits and comes off.

2. **Which** animal keeps water in its hump?

___ (a) The hippopotamus spends a lot of its time in the water.

___ (b) The camel's hump is where it keeps water for long trips.

___ (c) One kind of whale is called the humpback.

3. **What** helps a chick crack open its shell?

___ (a) A chick can crush itself by smashing its shell as it hatches.

___ (b) It takes a chick a long time to hatch from its shell.

___ (c) A chick's beak has a rock-like tip, which the chick can use to break its shell. The tip falls off when the chick is hatched.

4. **Where** do chipmunks make their nests?

___ (a) Chipmunks are rodents. They can be gray, brown, black, and even white.

___ (b) Chipmunks like to eat nuts and seeds. They stash them away to eat when they hibernate.

___ (c) Chipmunks like to live in trees. They make their nests of leaves and twigs in the branches.

The Hike

Read the story. Carefully follow Beth, Chip, and Shan's trail as you read. Later, you will fill in their trail on a map.

It was the month of May. The days were mild and warm. Beth, Chip, and Shan were going on a hike. As they set off they were thinking what fun they were going to have. They did not realize the shocks and knocks, and thrills and spills they'd meet on the way.

They hiked for a mile until Beth's shoes began to pinch her feet, making them bleed. They did not have any Band-Aids, so Beth had to grit her teeth and put up with the pain.

Next, Chip got a pain in his side from having too much in his backpack. He had to bend and stretch while Beth and Shan shifted some of his things into their backpacks.

They went on until they came to a steep hill. They were not used to backpacks and were finding it difficult to breathe. They wheezed and puffed until they got halfway up the hill.

There they came to a waterfall. They rushed to take a big drink. It was very refreshing.

Beth said, "Let's have lunch." So they unpacked their cheese sandwiches, chocolate cake, and lemonade. They began to eat, but many bugs began to bite them. They started to itch so much that they had to leave.

Still itching, they hiked along the trail until they came to a tree with wide branches that gave them shade from the sun. As they ate, they shared their meal with some chipmunks. Then they cleaned up and set off again.

Within minutes, Beth gave a shrill screech. "There's a snake!" she cried. A snake, at least three feet long, stretched across the path.

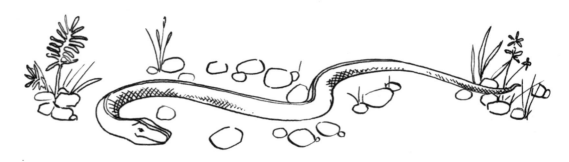

Beth was so shocked that she went as white as a sheet and began to shake. Chip dashed into the thick shrubs, and Shan went up the nearest tree. They all stayed still until the snake vanished into the brush.

The three of them continued on their way. Shan limped from a bruised leg, and Chip cleaned the scratches he had gotten in the shrubs.

The sun was still shining when they came to a forest. They followed the path in, but before long, they were lost.

They called and called to get help, but no one came.

"We'll just have to sit and wait until someone shows up," said Shan.

He had just finished speaking when there was a flash followed by a crash, and it began to rain. They did not have raincoats, so they got soaked. Wishing they were somewhere else, they hugged themselves to keep warm.

At last the rain stopped. Then there were footsteps on the path and a man and woman appeared between the trees. They had been in the forest many times and showed Beth, Chip, and Shan the way back. Before they left, the man and woman gave them some useful hiking tips.

As the three of them made their way back, they said, "The next time we go on a hike, we will have a plan!"

➜ Put an X next to the things you think Beth, Chip, and Shan should do the next time they go on a hike.

☐ Plan the trip and make a map of the trail.

☐ Take the map and a compass in case they get lost.

☐ Take a radio to listen to music.

☐ Take tent poles to keep up the tent.

☐ Pack Band-Aids.

☐ Take sunscreen to put on their skin so they do not get sunburned.

☐ Take bug spray to keep away the bugs.

☐ Pack nuts and grains to feed the animals.

☐ Take extra snacks and water.

➔ Reread the story and then draw a line of the trail that Beth, Chip, and Shan took.

LESSON 5: REVIEW OF CONSONANT TEAMS

Beth, Chip, and Shan would have had a better time if they had planned their hike. Make a plan for a trip you would like to take. It could be a trip to a nearby zoo or far away to another country. Write about the things you would need to take and three things you would do there.

When vowels are **followed by R**, they have an **unexpected sound** as in st**ar**.

star

Sound out the letters to read each word.

arm	car	card	dark
are	hard	park	harm
far	mark	part	jar
yard	cart	bark	art

start	shark	March	sharpen
starve	smart	carpet	garden
market	alarm	depart	chart
artist	darkness	arctic	marching

Learn to read this word: **heart**

➔ Use one of the words listed above to answer each riddle.
Write the word on the line.

1. A whole thing is made up of: _____s

2. A dog does this: _____

3. Your hand is at the end of it: _____

4. The stars appear when the sky is like this: _____

5. It's the opposite of soft: _____

6. It's a month of the year: _____

7. It's the opposite of near: _____

8. It means to begin: _____

→ Circle the name of the picture.

	far jar yard yarn		scarf starve start smart
	car cart chart card		hard harm charm alarm
	dark park part pardon		farm arm barn yarn
	car far jar star		arm alarm arctic artist

➜ Add **ar** to find out what each sentence is saying.

1. Taking off the b____k of a tree will h____m it.

2. It is h____d to see in the d____k.

3. "I'm st____ving. When can we st____t to eat?" asked Dara.

4. M____tha fell and broke her ____m.

5. M____c and Mac played in their y____d and then went to the p____k.

6. The f____m has a big b____n.

7. Dad had a h____d time st____ting his c____.

8. Ch____les's dog Star b____ked when the al____m went off.

➔ Read the sentence. Look at the word in bold print. Decide which meaning is best and then write **a** or **b**.

____ 1. Marsha Carlton was the school's **star** athlete.

____ 2. Art and Garth watched the **stars** shining in the dark.

     star = (a) best, main, well-known
               (b) a sun

____ 1. "These math problems are **hard**, but I did them!" said Martha.

____ 2. Nuts have **hard** shells to protect them.

     hard = (a) difficult
               (b) the opposite of soft

____ 1. The Carlsons are going to Martha's Vineyard in **March**.

____ 2. Bart is happy to be **marching** in the parade.

     March = (a) a month (b) to step, stride

____ 1. Charles jumped when the **alarm** went off.

____ 2. Mr. Barton was **alarmed** to find a deer in his garden eating his shrubs .

     alarm = (a) to be upset, shocked
                (b) a signal to put you on guard;
                    a clock that wakes you up

Stars of the Sea

Read the passage slowly and carefully so that you can remember all the details.

The stars of the sea are starfish. But you will find that they are not what they seem to be.

Circle the sentence you think is correct.

      (a) starfish are not shaped like stars

      (b) starfish are not fish

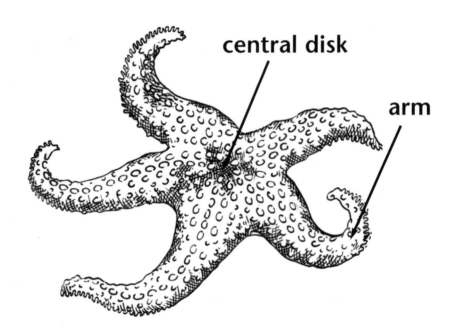

central disk

arm

If you've been to the beach, I bet you've seen starfish. But did you know that they are not fish?

A starfish is an animal with no backbone. Many starfish have five arms similar to a star, which is why they are called "starfish." But some have as many as fifty arms!

A starfish's arms grow from a hole that is named a central (sentral) disk. It is an opening to eat with, a stomach (stomack), and a brain.

Source: National Geographic *World*, August 1981.

Near the tip of each arm, the starfish has an eye spot. It does not see well with these eye spots. It cannot see shapes. It can just tell if it's dark.

→ Circle the correct answer.

1. Starfish are   (a) not shaped like stars   (b) not fish

2. Starfish have   (a) a backbone   (b) no backbone

3. Starfish have just five arms.
   (a) yes   (b) no, some have as many as fifty arms

4. Inside the central disk the starfish has
   (a) eye spots   (b) a brain

5. Near the tip of its arms the starfish has
   (a) eye spots   (b) an opening to eat with

6. The starfish can   (a) see well   (b) not see well

→ Reread the passage to see if your answers are correct. Then carefully read the passage on the next page to find out more about starfish.

Tube feet with
suction (suc-shun)
cups at the end

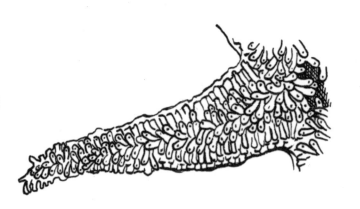

The bottom
of an arm

Sometimes you see a starfish with a missing arm. It may have broken off, but it may have been eaten. But this does not harm the starfish. It just grows back the missing arm!

Beneath the starfish's arms are rows and rows of small feet. In fact, there are hundreds of these tube-shaped feet. Each one ends in a small suction (suc-shun) cup. These help the starfish to pull itself along the bottom of the ocean and cling to rocks.

The starfish eats snails, clams, and mussels. The starfish opens a clam by pulling apart the shells with its arms.

There are many kinds of starfish. In fact, there are as many as 6,000! They may have been in the sea 500 million years ago.

Some starfish are the size of the end of your finger. But some grow to be three feet across. Wouldn't you be amazed if one of these big ones landed on a beach near you?

➜ Circle the correct answer.

1. If a starfish does not have 5 arms it means
   (a) it did not have five arms to begin with
   (b) an arm has broken off, but it may have been eaten

2. If a starfish has lost an arm, it will
   (a) die   (b) grow it back

3. Beneath a starfish's arm are
   (a) 5 feet   (b) hundreds of feet

4. The suction (suc-shun) cups beneath the starfish's arms
   (a) help it pull itself along the bottom of the ocean
   (b) stop it from pulling itself along the bottom of
        the ocean

5. The starfish eats   (a) clams   (b) seaweed

6. There are
   (a) many kinds of starfish
   (b) not many kinds of starfish

7. Starfish are   (a) all the same size   (b) many sizes

Did you get all the answers? Reread the passage and see.

✎ Find out about another animal of the sea and write about it. You can draw a picture, too.

_____

_____

_____

_____

_____

_____

_____

_____

_____

Lesson 7: Vowels with R: OR

When vowels are **followed by R**, they have an **unexpected sound** as in fork.

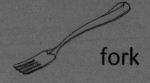 fork

Sound out the letters to read each word.

for	corn	sore	nor
core	more	cord	born
north	form	worn	horse
store	pork	port	sport

score	short	storm	torn
port	fort	forest	forget
effort	explore	report	before
forbid	morning	normal	record

Learn to read these words: your four pour
poor door floor hoarse board

➔ Match the words with their meanings.

_____ 1. explore   (a) a lot of trees
_____ 2. port   (b) to seek
_____ 3. forest   (c) where ships come, harbor

_____ 1. normal   (a) to stop
_____ 2. forbid   (b) where you shop
_____ 3. store   (c) usual, regular

_____ 1. afford   (a) dull
_____ 2. pour   (b) can pay
_____ 3. boring   (c) to let flow; to rain a lot

➜ Add **or** to find the name of each picture. Then write the number of the picture in the box.

☐ h____n

☐ th____n

☐ f____est

☐ raz____

☐ c____n

☐ h____se

☐ c____d

☐ st____m

☐ t____n

1.

2.

3.

4.

5.

6.

7.

8.

9.

➡ Find a word from the list to complete each sentence. Then write the word on the line.

1. "Please listen. This report is _____," said Ms. Stork.

   forbid

2. The class _____ the ruins of the fortress.

3. The rules _____ diving in the shallow end.

   port

   explored

4. When the storm came, they sailed into the _____.

   important

5. The storm began in the _____ and went on until dark.

   before

6. "It's quite _____ for a cut to be sore," said Dr. Lord.

   effort

7. "Please wipe your feet _____ coming into the kitchen," Dad said.

   normal

8. Chang made a big _____ and won the 100-yard dash.

   morning

➜ Write the correct word on the line.

1. Victor was late, and Lorna got _____ waiting for him.

2. Flora made a shelf from the _____.

   bored   board

3. Humans have _____s in their skin.

4. Dora _____ed some milk from the pitcher.

   pour   pore

5. The fans were _____ from yelling when their team scored.

6. Orlando rides his _____ each morning before school.

   horse   hoarse

7. Marc played the record for the _____th time.

8. Senator Orlo voted _____ the bill.

   four   for

➔ Read each sentence in bold print. Then put an X next to the sentence below it that has the same meaning.

1. **It's pouring cats and dogs.**

   ☐ Many cats and dogs have been born.

   ☐ Some cats and dogs fell from a jug.

   ☐ It's raining hard.

2. **I could eat a horse.**

   ☐ I would like a horse for lunch.

   ☐ I am starving.

   ☐ Long ago Americans used to eat horse meat.

3. **Don't let the cat out of the bag.**

   ☐ Do not tell the secret.

   ☐ Do not let the cat escape.

   ☐ Cats should be kept in bags.

4. **A stitch in time saves nine.**

   ☐ You should time yourself as you stitch.

   ☐ You should always make nine stitches.

   ☐ Effort in the beginning will save you time in the end.

The Wise Man

The man in this story was glad and grateful. Why do you think he was?

    (a) He lost all that he owned.

    (b) He became rich and could afford all that he desired.

    (c) He was given a motor boat.

Long ago, before the days of steamships and motorboats, a ship set sail from an Italian port. On board was a wise man who was a sailor.

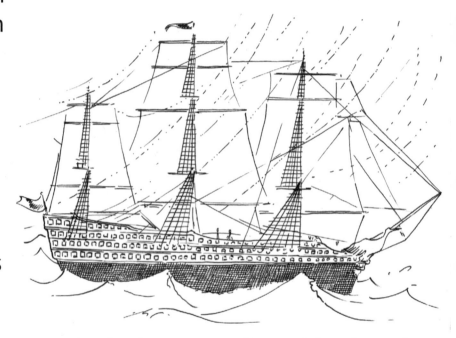

On the morning of the fourth day a bad storm arose. It became as dark as a forest. The sea became the color of black ink. The boat rocked. The cargo slipped back and forth. The men and women slid on the tilted deck.

In a short time, water began to fill the cabins. The wind tore into the sails. The mast broke and came crashing onto the deck.

The sailor began organizing the men and women into the lifeboats. It was hard, for they said they needed to bring their belongings with them.

"Forget your belongings. Leave your fortunes and fine clothes. Save yourselves!" the wise man yelled to them.

But they ignored him. Some said, "Leave them? Why, they are far too important to leave behind."

Before long the captain cried, "Abandon ship!"

The lifeboats were put into the sea, loaded down with the men and women and their belongings. But the wise man dived into the sea.

It was not long before the lifeboats sank. They had too much in them. The men and women sank, too, and were never seen again.

Meanwhile, the wise man held onto a board from the deck. In time he was swept ashore. He was glad and grateful that he had lost all that he had owned. By not taking his belongings, he had saved himself.

→ Reread the story to answer the questions. Circle the correct answer.

1. The sailor was wise to have
   (a) saved himself   (b) saved all his belongings

2. His shipmates were not wise, for they
   (a) did not get on the lifeboats and lost their lives
   (b) tried to save their belongings and lost their lives

3. What is the lesson of the story?
   (a) if you hang onto your belongings you will have a rich and full life
   (b) the most important thing you have is your life

Go back over the story and see how many words you can find with the **or** sound.

The wise man was indeed wise. He saved himself. See if you can make up three of your own wise or helpful sayings, such as "Think before you speak," "Great minds think alike," or "Try to do one good deed a day."

➔ Circle the name of the picture.

store star	form farm	sharpen shorten
cord card	reward record	stork start
born barn	part pour	dark door

→ Circle the missing letters. Then write them on the line.

1. Some plants have sh____p thorns to protect them.   ar   or

2. A harp and an ____gan are musical instruments.   ar   or

3. The N____th Star can guide you when you are at sea.   ar   or

4. Orlando had his portrait sketched by an ____tist.   ar   or

5. You don't need a c____ to go on short trips.   ar   or

6. It is normal for it to be d____k at four o'clock in the morning.   ar   or

7. Snorkeling is a great sp____t for those who like to swim.   ar   or

8. In a darts game you score by hitting a t____get.   ar   or

➔ Draw a line between the words that rhyme.

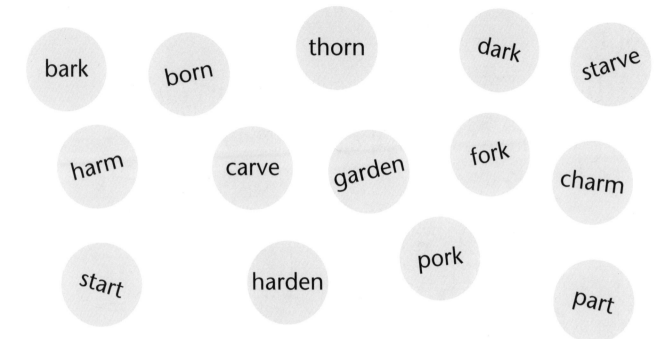

bark   born   thorn   dark   starve

harm   carve   garden   fork   charm

start   harden   pork   part

➔ Draw a line to the correct ending of each sentence.

1. Sharks' teeth are as sharp as   a rainbow.
2. An unripe plum is as tart as   a razor.
3. In March the crocus bulbs are as colorful as   a lemon.

4. Jarvis can be as hard to deal with as   a star.
5. The track star ran as fast as   the wind.
6. A diamond can shine like   a mule.

7. The shortcake was as hard as   a horse.
8. The cat's coat was as dark as   a rock.
9. Joe's hair was as long as the mane of   chocolate.

The Deer and the Lion

Read the story.

This is a Chinese story of a lion and a deer.
Lion-hearted means **brave.** Who is the lion-hearted one?
   (a) the lion   (b) the deer

One March morning a small deer was grazing by some park land when a lion appeared from the forest and came toward her.

The deer was so alarmed that she started to shake, and her heart beat fast.

"Oh dear, what am I going to do?" she asked herself.

She was quite alone and there was no escape. She made a big effort to be brave and waited.

A normal lion would have eaten the small deer in the wink of an eye. But this lion had never seen a deer before.

"What are those things growing next to your ears?" the lion asked.

"They're horns," replied the deer, thinking fast.

"What are horns used for?" asked the lion.

"Oh, they have an important job. They're used like a fork to stab lions," said the smart deer.

"You don't mean it?" said the lion in alarm. "And what are all those white marks on your chest and back?"

"You must not be very smart. All the animals know what they are for," replied the deer. "Each mark is for a lion I have eaten."

The lion became more alarmed, and he tore into the forest. There he met a fox.

➔ Checking up: see if you have followed the story. Circle the correct answer.

1. The month is April.   (a) yes   (b) no

2. The deer became alarmed.   (a) yes   (b) no

3. "Alarmed" means she was afraid.   (a) yes   (b) no

4. The lion tried to eat the deer.   (a) yes   (b) no

5. The lion asked the deer what her horns were used for.
    (a) yes   (b) no

6. The deer said her marks showed she had eaten some lions.   (a) yes   (b) no

"I've just met a fearsome animal who forks lions with her sharp horns and eats them," the lion said to the fox.

"A fearsome animal who forks lions and eats them!" repeated the fox. "Why, that must be the deer!" Then he gave a big grin and said, "Oh, what a trick she has played on you!"

"She did not trick me. No one tricks a lion!" said the lion.

"Well, she did," said the fox. Then he added, "If you'll lead me to the deer, I'll show you."

Before long they met up with the deer.

"Oh no!" the deer cried, "the fox must have given away my trick." She had to think fast.

"Hi, Fox!" she called. "Thank you. You're so kind to bring me such a fine lion like that to eat. You must have known that I'm starving."

When the lion heard this, he darted back into the forest. And the smart deer saved herself again!

➔ Circle the correct answer.

1. Lion-hearted means (a) brave   (b) mean

2. Who was lion-hearted?   (a) the deer   (b) the lion

3. When was the deer grazing in the park land?
   (a) in the morning   (b) in the evening

4. Why didn't the lion eat the deer in the wink of an eye?
   (a) he had just eaten
   (b) he had never seen a deer before

5. What did the deer say her horns were used for?
   (a) like a fork to stab lions
   (b) to reach the branches of tall trees

6. Who did the lion meet in the forest?
   (a) a wolf   (b) a fox

7. What did the deer do when the lion came back
   with the fox?
   (a) she darted into the forest
   (b) she tricked the lion again

✎ Write your own story about a brave animal.

LESSON 8: VOWELS WITH R: AR AND OR REVIEW

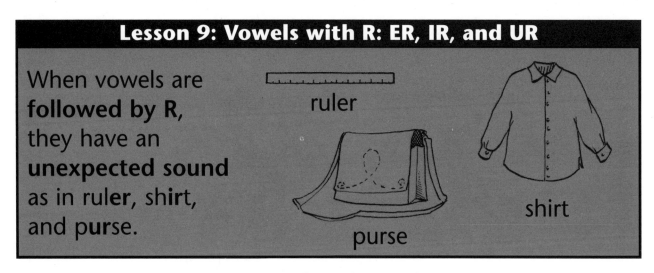

When vowels are **followed by R**, they have an **unexpected sound** as in rul**er**, sh**ir**t, and p**ur**se.

ruler

purse

shirt

Sound out the letters to read each word.

her	bird	burn	were
girl	hurt	jerk	fir
curl	dirt	fur	third
stern	stir	nurse	skirt

church	after	first	burst
summer	curtain	dessert	thirteen
curve	person	Thursday	better
birthday	hammer	surprise	northern

Learn to read this word that has the **er** sound: work

➔ Draw a line between the words that rhyme.

bird	herd	girl	first	burn	purse
stir	church	burst	letter	dirt	fern
perch	fur	better	curl	nurse	hurt

→ Circle the name of the picture.

burn barn	purse port	shirt shorts
board bored	nurse part	skirt scarf
porch park	third thirteen	far fir
perch pork	thirst Thursday	for first
better butter	torn turn	store stir
batter letter	learn burn	star stern

→ Circle the word that does not fit in each sentence.

1. The fans whispered to cheer on their team.

2. For dinner Pearl served hamburgers followed by dirt for dessert.

3. The girl perched on a branch of a birch tree and chirped a song.

4. Bert came first, Peter came two, Rupert was third, and Ernest was fourth.

5. Albert gave his sister, Irma, a church as a surprise birthday gift.

6. Ursula put her best summer hat on her elbow.

7. Kirk had such a thirst that he drank a whole glass of perfume.

8. Mervin got some dirt on his shirt so he put it in the washer to burn it.

We All Have Different Interests

➡ Find the correct meaning of the words in bold print. Then match the words with their meanings by writing the correct letter on the line next to each sentence.

(a) upset, bothered   (c) a clever, skillful person
(b) not expecting   (d) to come together, collect

_____ 1. Peter is into computers. He's spent so much time working with them that he's quite an **expert**.

_____ 2. Ernest likes surfboarding. He and his pals **gather** at the beach on the weekends and have a great time.

_____ 3. Marla is into reading. She does not like to be **disturbed** when she is reading a story.

_____ 4. Bert's favorite sport is basketball. He was **surprised** when he was picked for the school team.

➜ Match the words with their meanings.

_____ 1. reverse   (a) to go into

_____ 2. jerk   (b) to turn or go back

_____ 3. perch   (c) a sharp pull

_____ 4. enter   (d) to rest, sit on

_____ 1. stern   (a) up to date

_____ 2. swerve   (b) strict, harsh

_____ 3. curtains   (c) drapes

_____ 4. modern   (d) to turn aside, not go in a straight line

We All Have Different Lifestyles

➔ It is said that you can tell what a person is like by seeing her or his home. See if you can tell what Irma and Ursula's lifestyles are like from these pictures of their bedrooms.

This is Irma's bedroom.

This is Ursula's bedroom.

→ Read the sentences that tell about Irma's and Ursula's bedrooms. Put an **I** next to each sentence that tells about Irma's bedroom. Put a **U** next to each sentence that tells about Ursula's bedroom.

_____ She likes to surfboard.

_____ She likes snow sports.

_____ She likes casual clothes like shorts, skirts, and T-shirts.

_____ She has a thick, warm jacket and snow boots.

_____ She has a workbench and likes to make things with a hammer and nails.

_____ She has a desk where she can do homework.

_____ She does not have much furniture and does her homework perched on the bed.

_____ She has a pet bird, a parakeet.

_____ She has a pet dog named Tiger.

_____ She has short, plain curtains.

_____ She forgets where her things are and has a hard time finding them.

_____ She is neat and knows where all her things are.

→ Write the correct name on the line.

_____ lives in Florida where it is like summer all year long.

_____ lives in Vermont where there is a lot of snow in the winter.

✎ Describe what your bedroom is like.

_____

- -

_____

_____

- -

_____

_____

- -

_____

_____

- -

_____

_____

- -

_____

_____

- -

_____

When **AR** and **OR** come at the **end** of a word with more than one syllable, they usually have the **ER, IR, UR** sound as in dollar and visitor.

dollar   visitor

→ Choose a word from the list to complete each sentence. Write the word on the line.

elevator   dollar   collar   popular

1. Roberta likes to visit department stores so she can ride the _____.

2. Yesterday she paid four _____ s for a scarf.

3. Turner got a shirt with a colored _____.

4. The store is _____ with Roberta's classmates. It sells their favorite jeans.

We All Do Different Kinds of Work

➔ Read the sentences. Then write the number of the person that matches the sentence.

1. doctor   2. actor   3. operator   4. instructor

_____ This person teaches you things.

_____ This person likes to pretend to be different persons.

_____ This person makes something go.

_____ This person helps you when you are sick.

_____ This person teaches one student at a time.

_____ This person adds art to make what you read more fun.

_____ This person waves a stick and players of musical instruments follow him or her.

_____ This person checks to see that things are correct.

5. inspector   6. conductor   7. illustrator   8. tutor

What Am I?

Read the story and see if you can fill in the missing word. It has an **ar** ending with the **er** sound.

You've got a birthday coming up and you want to know which day of the week it will be on. What do you do? You go to a _____.

The _____ is the way we keep track of time. We have been using it for many years. It was invented by the Romans 2,000 years ago.

The _____ we use is called the Gregorian (Gre-gor-i-an) _____, and it is used by everyone.

The _____ divides the year into twelve months and keeps track of the seasons—spring, summer, fall, and winter. March always comes with the spring bulbs. June comes when the days are hot and full of sunshine. October arrives with the colorful reds and yellows of the tree's leaves. And Chanukah and Christmas are observed when it can freeze or even snow.

Each month is divided into weeks. And each week is divided into seven days. The days are Sunday, Monday, Tuesday, Wednesday, Thursday, Friday, and Saturday. There are 365 days in a year. That is a lot of days for birthdays!

The missing word is _____.

➜ Reread the story and then write in the correct answer.

1. There are _____ seasons.

2. There are _____ months in a year.

3. There are _____ days in a week.

4. Put the days of the week in the order they come.

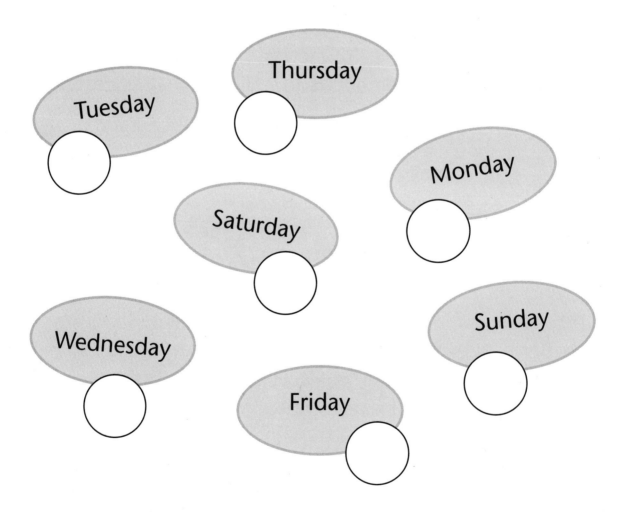

The calendar tells us the months of the year. Tell which is your favorite month and why you like it.

When vowels are **followed by R**, they have an **unexpected sound** as in **pear**.

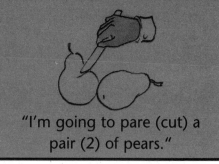

"I'm going to pare (cut) a pair (2) of pears."

Sound out the letters to read each word.

air	air	hair	fair	chair
	stair	flair	repair	despair

are   These words have the **"air" sound** when the **e** is silent:

bare	care	dare	fare
rare	stare	share	square
spare	glare	scare	aware
prepare	compare	careful	beware

ear   These words have the **"air" sound**:

pear	tear	wear
swear	bear	

Use this sentence to help you remember these words:

"I **swear** there was a **bear wearing** a coat with a **tear**, eating a **pear**."

→ Choose one of the words from the list on the right to find the answer to each sentence. Write the word on the line.

1. You breathe it all the time: _____

stair

2. You may go up these when you go to bed:
   _____ s

fare

3. It may be straight or it may curl: _____

wear

4. You pay this on the bus: _____

pear

5. You can eat it for a snack or dessert:

   _____

air

6. You do this to clothes: _____

hair

_____

7. You sit on it: _____

rare

8. Not usual: _____

tear

9. A rip in your shirt: _____

square

10. It has four sides of equal size: _____

spare

11. An extra part or thing: _____

fair

12. You go on rides at a _____

chair

→ Circle the words that have the same sound but different spellings and meanings. Then put an X next to the sentence that tells about the picture. The first one is done for you.

☐ Peter ran up the (stairs) to get his sneakers.

☒ Norman (stared) at the cupcakes in the store window.

☐ Clare got her bus fare from her purse before the bus came.

☐ Pearl is wearing her fair hair in braids.

☐ When Mrs. Hubbard got there, the cupboard was bare.

☐ It is rare to see a black bear these days.

☐ Lin went to the hardware store to get a hammer.

☐ Ernest is wearing a pair of jeans that has a square patch over a tear.

Up in the Air—Before Jets

Read the story.

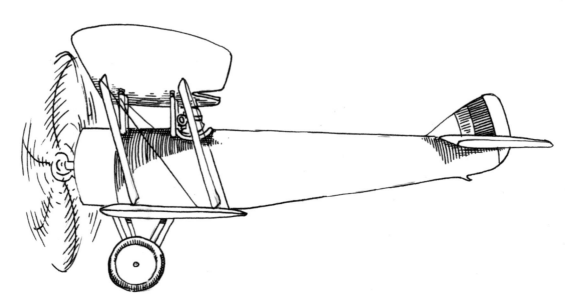

Many of the first airplanes had two wings
and were called biplanes.

When we go to an airport today, we see many jets, endless concrete runways, and tall structures that track the airplanes by radar. But what were airplanes and airports like fifty years ago?

A lot different, that's for sure! First, many of the first airplanes had open cockpits. You had to wear thick clothes and a helmet to protect yourself from the wind. You needed goggles (gog-guls) to protect your eyes. And you had to wear strong straps to keep you in your seat.

Second, the first planes did not have many instruments. It was unusual to have a radio. Pilots depended on their eyes to find their way and to locate other airplanes. Even if a pilot had a radio it was not a great deal of help. It was rare for an airport to have radio control!

Source: National Geographic *World,* Sept. 1981.

Landing and taking off were also difficult. The airports were just strips of grassland.

The first planes were slower and not as streamlined as modern airplanes. Some were all metal. Others had wings made from lumber and fabric.

Coming in to land. Pilots landed on grass runways. They did not have radios and had to depend on their eyes and skill to land.

They were hard to pilot in strong winds. But they could do things modern airplanes cannot. They could hover like helicopters, glide, and turn, so they could do difficult and complicated air stunts.

Would you like to pilot one of the first planes? Do you think it would be fun or would you be scared?

Seeing the world from the other side! A pilot is turning over his plane in an air stunt. Strong straps keep him in!

→ Circle the correct answer.

1. Piloting one of the first planes was ____ than piloting a modern jet.
   (a) easier and safer   (b) harder and not as safe

2. The first pilots had to wear
   (a) colorful clothes so they could be seen
   (b) thick clothes to protect them from the wind

3. The first pilots landed by
   (a) using their eyes   (b) using their radios

4. The first planes landed on
   (a) concrete runways   (b) grass runways

5. Do you think it would be more fun to
   (a) pilot a modern jet
   (b) pilot one of the first planes

✎ Flying—and all travel—were very different fifty years ago. Tell what you think it will be like to travel in the future.

→ Circle the name of the picture.

hair horn hurt hat	stare start stairs star	shore shirt short share
wear watch word wink	ham hatch hard horse	torn tear turn tart
corn cart can care	patch pare perch part	bark bear bake burn
pack pocket park porch	storm stir store start	herd hare hard heart

→ Draw a line between the words that rhyme.

thorn born	farm dare	share sport
square curve	pear harm	star tear
swerve fair	stair scare	short jar
hurt part	starve store	care bear
care fare	purse carve	heart scorch
cart skirt	more curse	porch start

→ Read the sentence and circle the missing word. Write the word on the line.

1. "Let's give Robert a surprise party for his birthday on the _____ of March," said Kamar.

   three   third   thirteen

2. For dessert Martha served ripe _____ and custard.

   pares   pairs   pears

3. The car swerved as Arthur missed his turn. He was not _____ but it gave him a scare.

   alarmed   torn   hurt

4. "Are you _____ that your homework was due last Thursday?" asked Mr. Birch, glaring at Peter.

   aware   care   stare

5. Bertha likes to keep her hair _____ in the summer.

   shirt   short   sharp

6. "I like Saturdays," said Carmen. "In the morning I go to the _____ and then to the park."

   stair   store   star

→ Put an X in the box next to the correct answer to the question

1. **What makes a dirty mark on the carpet?**
   ☐ (a) walking over it in your bare feet
   ☐ (b) spilling a pitcher of water on it
   ☐ (c) a dog running in from the garden on a wet day

2. **Which needs to be repaired?**
   ☐ (a) a pair of shoes that have dirt on them
   ☐ (b) a chair with a straight back that is missing a leg
   ☐ (c) a car with no spare tire

3. **Which is the hardest?**
   ☐ (a) a frozen cube of water left in the sun for a day
   ☐ (b) a crisp cracker dunked into a hot cup of chocolate
   ☐ (c) a bag of dried-up marshmallows

4. **Which is the sharpest?**
   ☐ (a) the feather end of an arrow
   ☐ (b) a bit of broken glass
   ☐ (c) a pair of scissors with blunt ends

The Snowgirl

Read the story.

This story tells of a husband and wife who lived in Russia many years ago. More than anything else, they wanted a child. In time they got a child, but she was different from normal children.

Why do you think she was different?

(a) She disappeared for part of each year.
(b) She never came back.

It was winter again and Ednar and Igor were sadder than ever. Another year had passed and they still had not become parents.

"It is sad we do not have a child," Ednar said one morning as she pulled back the curtains and stared at some children having fun in the snow, making a snowman.

Then she cried in despair, "It's not fair! After thirteen years you'd think we'd have a child."

"Yes, dear, it does seem unfair," agreed Igor. "Then, to cheer her up, he said, "Say, why don't we go and make a snowman?"

"Okay," said Ednar, "but let's make a snowgirl!"

They went into the garden and started to make a snowgirl. They worked hard and, by the end of the morning, they had made a charming girl from the snow. They dressed her in the garments they had been saving for their child. They added the long, fair braids that Ednar had worn long ago, before she cut her hair short.

They were admiring their work when, much to their surprise, the snowgirl smiled and waved her arms at them. Then she turned, marched toward the door of their hut, and went inside.

Ednar and Igor ran after her. The snowgirl was sitting in a chair as if she had come to stay.

➡ Checking up: see if you have followed the story. Circle the correct answer.

1. Ednar and Igor had been wed for fourteen years.
   (a) yes   (b) no

2. Ednar and Igor made a snowman. (a) yes   (b) no

3. They finished by the end of the morning. (a) yes   (b) no

4. Ednar had short hair. (a) yes   (b) no

5. The snowgirl ran into the hut. (a) yes   (b) no

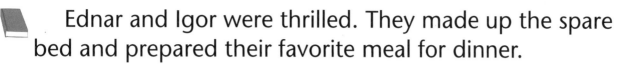

Ednar and Igor were thrilled. They made up the spare bed and prepared their favorite meal for dinner.

The snowgirl stayed. She became more and more beautiful. And Igor and Ednar became more and more fond of her.

The days passed until winter came to an end and spring arrived. The sun came out. The waters in the frozen river began to flow. All the children and their parents were cheerful and glad. All, that is, but the snowgirl. She sat curled up on her favorite chair in a dark corner of the hut, ignoring Ednar and Igor's pleas to play in the sun with the other children.

"What is the matter, dear child?" Ednar asked. "Are you sick? Are you hurt?"

But all the girl would say was, "It's nothing."

Summer arrived. The sun became hotter, and the children spent more and more time playing in the sunshine.

One day the girls went for a walk. They called to the snowgirl, "Come with us!"

But the snowgirl was afraid to leave the hut.

"It is too hot, and there's too much glare from the sun," she said.

But Ednar said, "Go, dear child. You spend too much time alone."

And Igor said, "Yes, do go."

The snowgirl wanted to please her parents, so she went. But while the others played in the sun, she sat under a big birch tree, dangling her feet in a stream.

When evening came and the sun set, the girls started to shiver. So they made a bonfire and sat beside it. Then they played a game, jumping over the fire. First one jumped, then another, and then a third.

When it was the snowgirl's turn, she hung back.

"Why don't you jump? Don't you dare?" the other girls asked, teasing her.

The snowgirl was scared. But she did not want the girls to go back and tell her parents she was a bad sport. So she clenched her fists, ran toward the fire, and jumped.

→ Checking up: see if you are still following the story. Circle the correct answer.

1. Ednar and Igor prepared dinner. (a) yes (b) no

2. The snowgirl began to melt. (a) yes (b) no

3. When the sun came out, everyone was glad but the snowgirl. (a) yes (b) no

4. The snowgirl hid in her bedroom. (a) yes (b) no

5. The snowgirl was afraid to leave the hut. (a) yes (b) no

6. The snowgirl wanted to please her parents.
   (a) yes (b) no

7. The children made a fire. (a) yes (b) no

8. The snowgirl was scared and did not jump over the fire
   (a) yes (b) no

The girls stared in horror—where was the snowgirl? She had disappeared! All that was left was a white mist that rose up, up, and up into the air.

Poor Ednar and Igor were heartbroken when their dear snowgirl did not return that evening. They waited and waited but she did not come back.

They were sadder than ever and talked of nothing but the dear child. They cared for her so much.

After a while the days became shorter. The sun lost its warmth, the air became brisk, and winter returned.

One morning, when the first snow was falling, there was a tap, tap, tapping at Ednar and Igor's window.

They went to see what it was. There, smiling and sparkling in the snow, was their dear snowgirl. They were together again, at last! She stayed all winter helping Ednar and Igor with the chores and playing with the other children.

When the days became longer and the sun became stronger, the snowgirl disappeared again. But this time, Ednar and Igor were not so sad. They realized that each winter when it started to snow, their dear child would return to them, and she would bring them all the happiness they could wish for.

➜ Circle the correct answer.

1. Why was the snowgirl different from the other children?
   (a) she disappeared for part of each year
   (b) she never came back

2. Why were Ednar and Igor so sad the first time the snowgirl disappeared?
   (a) they did not know she would return
   (b) they needed her to do the chores

3. Why were they not so sad the next time the snowgirl disappeared?
   (a) she said she'd return before winter came
   (b) they realized she would return each winter

4. The snowgirl was
   (a) brave for risking her life
   (b) not smart for risking her life

Write your own story about a snowman, snowboy, or snowgirl who comes alive.

_____

- -

_____

- -

_____

- -

_____

- -

_____

- -

_____

- -

_____

- -

_____

- -

_____

Lesson 12: Syllables

A word has as many syllables as it has **vowel sounds**.	1	thick, st**a**r**e**
	2	chick-en, re-cord
	3	wheel-bar-row, im-por-tant
	4	re-pol-ish-ing, com-par-i-son

Remember: There is only **one vowel sound** when:
- There is a **silent e** (cake).
- Two vowels come together and the **first** one is **long** and the **second** is **silent** (rain).

→ Circle the vowels. Write the number of vowels in each word. Then write the number of vowel sounds and syllables in the word.

	Vowels	Vowel sounds & Syllables		Vowels	Vowel sounds & Syllables
corn	_____	_____	birthday	_____	_____
girl	_____	_____	lunch	_____	_____
surprise	_____	_____	garden	_____	_____
north	_____	_____	chop	_____	_____
Thanksgiving	_____	_____	breathe	_____	_____
child	_____	_____	compare	_____	_____
shadow	_____	_____	selfish	_____	_____
explore	_____	_____	smart	_____	_____
Saturday	_____	_____	furniture	_____	_____
channel	_____	_____	while	_____	_____
starve	_____	_____	summer	_____	_____
before	_____	_____	support	_____	_____
width	_____	_____	Thursday	_____	_____
hamburger	_____	_____	heart	_____	_____
nothing	_____	_____	cheerful	_____	_____

→ Draw a line between the beginning and end of each word.

sum	part
cloth	mer
shal	ing
de	low

chip	port
rub	pet
car	bish
re	munk

thank	ner
part	ful
sum	day
birth	mer

ex	thing
sur	pare
any	prise
com	plore

chop	get
be	sticks
dark	fore
for	ness

mean	ware
be	while
re	ter
let	pair

teach	ing
but	ish
van	ter
wear	er

win	ow
shad	ter
care	or
col	ful

When two words are put together to make one word, it is called a **compound word**. Divide a compound word between the two words.

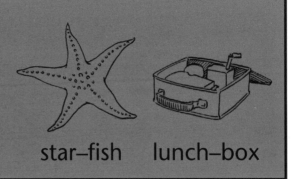

star–fish   lunch–box

→ Use a slash mark to divide each compound word between the two words.

shortcut	lampshade	chopsticks	birdbath
thunderstorm	birthday	wheelbarrow	heartbroken
cheesecake	shellfish	stairway	sunburn
sparkplug	raincoat	bathtub	airplane
Thanksgiving	something	homework	mailbox

→ Choose a compound word from the list above to complete each sentence.

1. Althea put Spot into the _____ to get him clean.

2. Mom made a _____ for Peter's birthday.

3. Robert and Tomasa are planning to come home for _____.

4. Never stay under a tree in a _____.

5. "I know there is _____ I've forgotten," said Koreen, running back to the store to get milk.

6. Charles stayed too long in the sunshine and got a _____.

7. "The car won't go. I think there is something the matter with the _____," said Dad.

8. Martha was _____ when her pet rabbit died.

The Soup Stone

Read the story, which is a retelling of an old tale.

Learn to read these words: **soup salt**

One winter morning a man was returning home from a long trip. There was a chill wind, and his clothes were thin and worn. He'd had nothing to eat for some time.

"What I need is some hot **soup**," he said as he pulled his coat collar up to his chin and tried to stop shivering.

At last he came to a home where a family was preparing dinner. The man asked if they could spare him something to eat. But they said, "No, we cannot spare you anything."

"Well, have you got a big pot?" the man asked.

"Yes, we have a big pot," the wife said. And she fetched it from a kitchen shelf.

"Do you have water?" he asked.

"Yes," said the husband. "We have water."

"Pour four jugs of water into the pot and put it on the fire," said the man, "for I have a **soup** stone with me."

"A **soup** stone? Whatever is that?" the husband, the wife, and their children asked in surprise. They had never seen such a thing before.

"It's a stone that makes **soup**," explained the man, taking a stone from his pocket.

They stared at the stone as he turned it over in his hand. It did not seem any different from a **regular** stone.

With great care, the man polished the stone on a cloth. Then he tossed it into the pot that the wife had filled with water and put on the burning fire.

"We must heat up the water," he said.

When the water was bubbling, the man said, "Can we add a pinch of **salt**?"

"Yes, we can," said the wife, and she fetched a jar of **salt**.

The man put some **salt** into the pot. Then they all pulled up chairs and sat next to the pot to watch it.

"Don't you think an onion would add to the flavor?" asked the man.

"Run next door to Mrs. Storch for an onion," the husband said to the first child. The child dashed next door and before long returned with three onions. She peeled and chopped them up, and stirred them into the pot.

"A carrot or two will add to the taste," **remarked** the man.

"Oh, we've got some carrots," said the wife, and she got some from under a bench. The wife cleaned and chopped up the carrots and put them into the pot.

They continued to watch the pot and chatted until the man said, "It's a shame we don't have any potatoes to thicken up the **soup**."

"We've got some potatoes," said the eldest girl. "I'll get them."

She rushed off to the barn where the potatoes were stored and she returned with a handful. Then she scrubbed them, cut them up, and put them in the pot.

→ Checking up: see if you are following the story. Circle the correct answer.

1. The man had been away a long time. (a) yes   (b) no

2. The man was hungry. (a) yes   (b) no

3. The man asked them if they had a microwave.
   (a) yes   (b) no

4. They poured in three jugs of water. (a) yes   (b) no

5. The family had not seen a soup stone before.
   (a) yes   (b) no

6. The man polished the stone. (a) yes   (b) no

7. After putting the stone in the water, the man first asked for some pepper. (a) yes   (b) no

8. They put some corn into the pot. (a) yes   (b) no

9. They got some onions from Mrs. Storch. (a) yes   (b) no

As they waited for the **soup**, they shared tales and jokes.

"I remember that my parents used to grow turnips. They were great in **soup**," the man said.

"Why, we're growing turnips," exclaimed the wife. She said to the third child, "Run into the garden and dig up some turnips." The child ran into the garden and returned with **several** fresh turnips. They washed off the dirt, **pared** them, and stirred them into the pot.

"It won't be long," said the man as they got a **whiff** of a **tempting** smell. "Say, a dash of pepper will give the **soup** an extra something. Do you have any?"

"Yes, we do," said the wife, and she fetched some and stirred it in.

Just then, Peter, the eldest son, returned from hunting. He had two hares. "What have you got there?" the son asked, nodding toward the pot. "The smell is great, and I'm starving."

"It's **soup**. We have a visitor and he's making us some **soup** from a **soup** stone he has," said his dad.

The man smiled at Peter and said, "Greetings." Then he said, "Those hares are just what we need to finish off the **soup**."

And before anyone could say "**soup** stone," he whisked away the hares, skinned them, chopped them, and put them into the pot.

At last the **soup** was done. There was so much **soup** that they could not have eaten one bite of dessert if there had been any.

"It's the richest **soup** I've ever had!" exclaimed the husband as he finished his serving.

"We'd like some more!" said the children.

The wife said, "Thank you so much. It's the best meal we've had for a long time."

"Yes, I like it, too," said the man. "And the stone will make **soup** like this forever if you do what we did today." Then he smiled at the wife and said, "You may keep the stone. I do not need it."

"Oh, that is not fair," the wife started to say. But the man cut her short and said, "It's nothing."

Then he gathered up his things, bade them farewell, and left.

He went on his way. He was in luck. He came upon another stone just before he came to some new homes.

This stone worked just as well as the first one. In fact, all the stones he used worked just as well.

→ Checking up: see if you have followed the story. Circle the correct answer.

1. The fourth child got the turnips.
   (a) yes   (b) no

2. The eldest son came home with two hares.
   (a) yes   (b) no

3. The man chopped up the hares before the family had time to say anything.
   (a) yes   (b) no

4. The soup was the best soup they had ever had.
   (a) yes   (b) no

5. "Cut her short" means that the man did not let the wife finish what she was saying.
   (a) yes   (b) no

6. The man went off with the stone.
   (a) yes   (b) no

7. The man never got a stone like that again.
   (a) yes   (b) no

→ Reread the story if you think you need to. Then circle the correct answer.

1. The story tells of a man who
   (a) made soup from nothing but a stone
   (b) used a stone to show that if you're smart and use what you have, you will not starve

2. It was   (a) summer   (b) winter

3. When the man asked the family if they'd share their dinner, they said
   (a) "We cannot spare you anything."
   (b) "Go away, do not bother us."

4. The man first asked: (a) "Do you have a fire?"
   (b) "Do you have a big pot?"

5. The stone   (a) shone and glittered
   (b) did not seem any different from a regular stone

6. Put the sentences in the order they come in the story:
   _____ (a) "Can we add a pinch of salt?"
   _____ (b) "Do you have water?" he asked.
   _____ (c) The child ran into the garden and returned with several fresh turnips.
   _____ (d) "It's a shame we don't have any potatoes."

7. Could the man have made the soup if he had not had the stone?   (a) yes   (b) no

8. Why did the other stones work as well as the first stone?
   (a) It was not the stones but all the other things the man added that made the soup.
   (b) The man always polished the stones well before he put them into the pot.

➔ Find these words in the story. Then match the words with their meanings.

several   regular   whiff
tempting   pared   remarked

_____ 1. several	(a) usual, normal	
_____ 2. regular	(b) more than two, but not many	
_____ 3. whiff	(c) a puff, a wave of a smell	

_____ 1. pared	(a) said	
_____ 2. tempting	(b) cut up	
_____ 3. remarked	(c) something you would like	

➔ Use one of the words from the list above to complete each sentence.

1. "What size hamburger would you like, a _____ or a jumbo?" asked Nick.

2. A _____ smell came from the kitchen.

3. Robert got a _____ of the chocolate cake when Mom opened the oven door.

4. _____ birds were perched on the branch of the birch tree.

5. "We will need umbrellas for it is starting to rain," _____ Hakim.

6. Chester _____ the pear and ate it.

✎Write your own story about a special or magical stone.

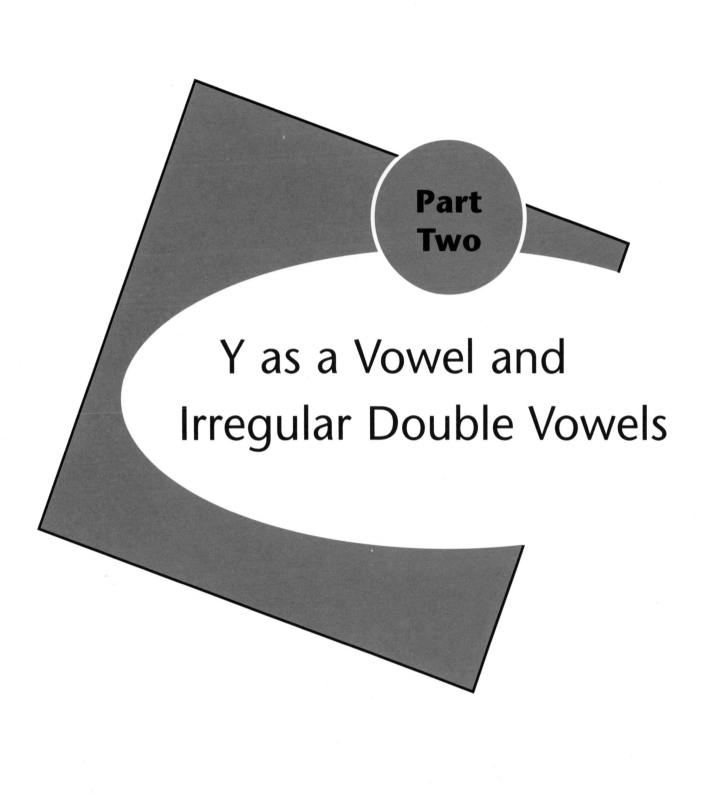

Part Two

Y as a Vowel and
Irregular Double Vowels

Lesson 14: Y as a Vowel

Y is always a **vowel** when it comes at the **end of a word.** When **Y** is the **only vowel** at the end of a **one-syllable** word, it has the **long i** sound as in cry.

When **Y** is the **only vowel** at the end of a word with **more than one syllable**, it has the **long e** sound as in candy.

cry

candy

Sound out the letters to read each word.

long i	my	by	try	sky
	fly	fry	sly	dry
	why	spy	shy	spry
	pry	ply	cry	sty

long e	happy	baby	funny	sleepy
	party	puppy	slowly	tiny
	dirty	soapy	shady	thirty
	stormy	pony	curly	lately
	daily	slippery	every	family
	history	finally	story	carefully

→ Draw a line between the words that rhyme.

why	dirty	funny	weepy	spy	sty
thirty	cry	sleepy	sky	slyly	tasty
slowly	holy	try	sunny	hasty	shyly

➜ Circle the name of the picture.

cry　　　　fry	my　　　　　by	pry　　　　dry
spry　　　fly	why　　　ply	try　　　　by
shy　　　sty	try　　　　fry	ply　　　　pry
sky　　　sly	dry　　　　fly	sly　　　spy

➜ Match the words with their meanings.

_____ 1. shy　　　(a) cunning, crafty

_____ 2. sly　　　(b) lively, quick

_____ 3. spry　　　(c) bashful, timid

_____ 1. pry　　　(a) a pig pen

_____ 2 fry　　　(b) to peek into; to raise, pull open

_____ 3. sty　　　(c) a way of cooking

→ Choose a word from the list below to complete each sentence. Write the word on the line.

shy   sly   spry   pry   fry   sty

1. It is rude to _____ into another person's secrets.

2. Billy is so _____ that he won't come to Vinay's birthday party.

3. If someone is _____ you say that she or he is as cunning as a fox.

4. "I will _____ the eggs when I have made the toast," said Jamel.

5. Although Mrs. Reddy is quite elderly, she is still _____ and full of life.

6. Every day Valery goes to the _____ to feed her pigs.

→ **Add y to find the name of each picture. Then write the number of the picture in the box.**

☐ pon__

☐ thirt__

☐ dais__

☐ cand__

☐ bab__

☐ fl__

☐ penn__

☐ pupp__

☐ butterfl__

1.

2.

3.

4.

5.

30

6.

7.

8.

9.

→ Choose one of the **y** words with the **long e** sound to answer each riddle. Write the word on the line.

1. When we are tired we are _____.   penny

2. It comes after twenty-nine: _____

3. We all start life as one: _____   baby

4. If you do something every day, you do it
   _____.   thirty

5. Kim carefully
   counted each   daily
   _____
   before he put it in
   his piggy bank.   sleepy

                                                       funny
6. A great joke is this: _____

7. Parents and children make up a   every
   _____.

8. You can ride it: _____   slowly

9. At last! _____   finally

10. Not very big: _____   family

11. It means all, each: _____   pony

12. Not fast: _____   tiny

→ Read the name of each picture. Then circle all the words
that have the same **y** sound as the picture.

candy	happy forty fry windy why
fly	by barely lady sly try
cherry	my funny tidy try curly
spy	quickly ply penny shiny shy
penny	slowly sly crafty plenty by

➔ Read each sentence and circle the missing word.

1. Kenny was happily _____ his kite when the wind suddenly whisked it into the sky.

   trying   flying

2. "Try to step _____. It rained and the path is very wet and slippery," warned Shibly.

   carefully   carelessly

3. Kirby _____ baby-sits for the Penny family.

   regularly   really

4. "Why don't we find a shady spot where it is not so _____," said Kelly.

   funny   sunny

5. Mrs. Finlay does her _____ chores before nine-thirty every morning.

   daily   dairy

6. "I don't know _____ we can't pry this box open," Peggy said crossly.

   by   why

Solve the Mystery!

📕 Read each passage slowly and carefully.

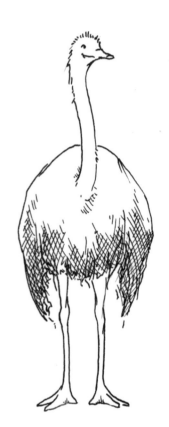

Which bird can't fly?

You wouldn't have a hard time spying this bird if you happened to visit the African plains. It has a long neck that can reach the top of a tree that is 8 feet in size. In fact, the ostrich is the biggest bird there is. But unlike other birds, it cannot fly. It has to rely on its strong legs to escape an enemy.

➡ Circle the correct answer.

1. This bird can be seen in
   (a) America (b) Africa

2. This bird may be as big as a tree that is
   (a) 8 feet in size (b) 18 feet in size

3. This bird is (a) the tiniest there is (b) the biggest there is

4. An ostrich cannot fly, but it escapes from an enemy by
   (a) putting its head in the sand (b) running

Why can a fly travel up the side of your home?

You can surely tell when it's summer! You're hot, sticky, and probably thirsty, and there's a fly buzzing near your ear that is bothering you. You run inside and carefully close the screen door, but the sly creature usually beats you to it.

Flies are dirty creatures, but you must admit that they are crafty and clever. What creature do you know that can travel up the side of your home? Actually, it's not at all hard for flies to do this. They have tiny suction (suc-shun) cups on their six feet that can stick to nearly anything.

→ Circle the correct answer.

1. Flies bother us mainly in (a) the winter (b) the summer

2. Flies are (a) dirty (b) clean

3. Flies have (a) four feet (b) six feet

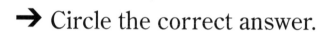

Where does a butterfly come from?

You could hardly see it. But there, on the underside of the leaf, hidden from the summer sun, was a tiny greenish egg.

Nearly a week later the egg hatched into a tiny green larva, or what you and I would call a caterpillar.

The caterpillar hid under the leaves and slowly ate them. It shed its skin five times, each time getting bigger, until one day it hung on the underside of a leaf. There it became a hard, dark, dry pupa.

After two to three weeks the pupa split open, and inside was a beautiful butterfly. It beat its wings rapidly to dry them before flying away.

➔ Circle the correct answer.

1. The tiny egg was (a) a dark color   (b) a greenish color

2. The egg hatched into a caterpillar after nearly
    (a) a week   (b) a month

3. The caterpillar hid (a) under the leaves
    (b) in a hole in a tree trunk

4. On the underside of a leaf, the caterpillar turned into
    (a) a larva   (b) a pupa

5. The butterfly first (a) beat its wings to dry them
    (b) beat its wings to fly away

Find out about a bird, an animal, or an insect. Then write about what makes it special.

When words ending in **Y** add an ending, they drop the **Y** and keep their **long i** and **long e** sounds.

dry + ed = dried   try + s = tries
silly + est = silliest   happy + ness = happiness

→ Circle the words that dropped the **y** when an ending was added to them. Then put an **i** over the circled words with the **long i** sound, and an **e** over the circled words with the **long e** sound. The first one is done for you.

☐ Lenya (pried) open the can of cranberry jelly.

☐ Patty fried the hamburgers too long, and they were very dry.

☐ There were two babies in the buggy, Betty and Becky.

☐ A baby bird tries to fly by flapping its wings.

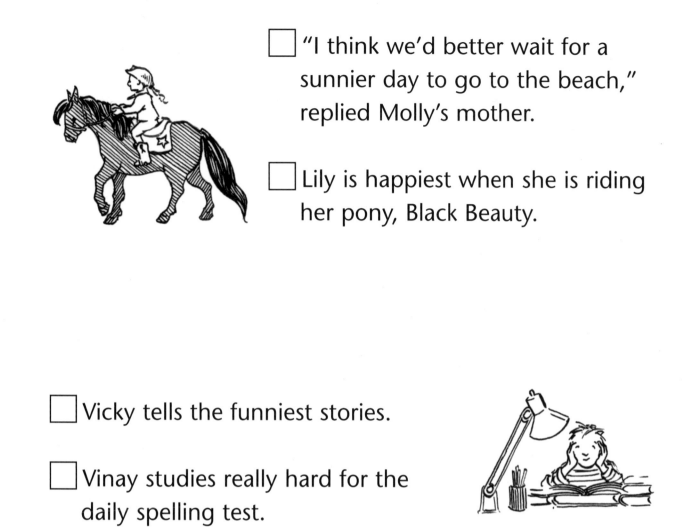

☐ "I think we'd better wait for a sunnier day to go to the beach," replied Molly's mother.

☐ Lily is happiest when she is riding her pony, Black Beauty.

☐ Vicky tells the funniest stories.

☐ Vinay studies really hard for the daily spelling test.

➔ Now go back and put an X in the box next to the sentence that tells about the picture.

The Camel's Nose

Read this story from Arabia about a man and his camel. What lesson do you think the story teaches?

Learn to read this word: **front**

One chilly evening a sleepy and tired man was preparing to go to bed in his tent after a long trip.

"My, I'm lucky to have such a warm and cozy tent to sleep in on such a chilly evening," he was happily saying to himself, when his camel suddenly stuck his nose under the flap of the tent.

"Master," the camel said, "do you mind if I put my nose inside the tent? It's extremely chilly and my nose is freezing."

The man was naturally surprised, but he replied, "Very well. You may put your nose inside the tent."

The camel quickly poked his nose into the tent. A short time later, the camel said, "Dear Master, please may I put my neck into the tent? I may catch a chill if the top part of me is warm and my neck is not."

The man did not like the idea of having the camel put his

long neck into his tent. But he felt badly for the camel. So he replied, "Very well. You may put your neck into the tent."

An even shorter time later, the camel said, "Fine Master, please let me put my **front** legs into the tent. I'm sleepy and it's very hard to get to sleep when I'm standing this way."

"Very well," said the man. "You may put your **front** legs into the tent."

The tent was not very big, so the man shifted over to one side so that the camel could get his **front** legs into the tent.

Next, the camel cried, "Please, great Master, let the rest of me into the tent. For I am keeping the flap open and the chilly air is pouring in."

"Very well," the man said unhappily, "you may bring the rest of your body inside."

The camel quickly pushed his way inside the tent. But it was too tiny for the two of them.

"I don't think that the tent will keep the two of us warm," the camel said to his master. "You are not as big as I am, so you had better leave."

Then the camel gave the man a big push and, before the man could say "a camel's nose," he was outside and shivering in the darkness.

He stared sadly at the tent with its flap carefully pulled across the opening and said, "I can see that it's better to stop some things before they get started!"

→ Circle the correct answer.

1. What is the lesson of the story?
   (a) if you have a frozen nose you will get your way
   (b) it's better to stop some things before they get started

2. The camel got into the tent
   (a) quickly, by pushing in his whole body before the man could say no.
   (b) slowly, by getting in one part of his body after another.

3. The camel was (a) sly (b) shy

4. The man was (a) too helpful (b) too angry

The man in this story was tricked by a camel. Write a story about a person or an animal who plays a trick on someone else.

_____

_____

_____

_____

_____

_____

_____

_____

_____

_____

_____

_____

_____

_____

_____

_____

_____

_____

_____

_____

Lesson 15: Irregular Double Vowel OO as in Moon

When the **vowels OO** come together, they have an **unexpected sound** as in m**oo**n.

moon

Sound out the letters to read each word.

soon	food	room	cool
boot	roof	hoop	root
pool	too	noon	fool
tooth	shoot	zoo	choose

ooze	loose	stool	tool
droop	gloom	snooze	broom
school	foolish	smooth	bloom
shampoo	bedroom	cartoon	balloon

➔ Circle the words that rhyme with the word in the box.

school	pool	soon	fool	zoo	tool
ooze	snooze	goose	roof	stool	choose
room	bloom	booth	broom	gloom	noon
boot	tooth	shoot	droop	root	soon
loop	snoop	hoop	food	droop	boot

→ Circle the name of the picture.

root room roof rook	tool tooth tall tune
moose move mood goose	boat bowl boot beat
zoo too igloo loom	drop droop stool stoop
raccoon cocoon balloon cartoon	spook spoke shoe spoon

➜ Circle the missing letter. Then write the letter on the line.

1. A __oose is sometimes eaten at Thanksgiving.   m   g   l

2. You can tell a __accoon by the rings on its tail.   c   b   r

3. You can only see a kangaroo in America if you go to the __oo.   s   z   t

4. If a plant does not get water it will ____oop.   sn   tr   dr

5. The hill was steep and Ted was foolish not to wear his hiking __oots.   h   b   f

6. If you put air into a __alloon it will expand.   b   g   l

7. A male chicken is called a __ooster.   b   m   r

8. We eat the __oots of some plants, such as carrots, potatoes, turnips, and parsnips.   f   t   r

Solve the Mystery: 2

Sung Soo had the afternoon off from school, so she and her mother went to the zoo. But Sung and her mother had a big surprise when they got home—for it was a mess!

Had a burglar broken in? Or had there been some other visitor?

Study the picture carefully and see if you can find some clues to tell what happened, who did it, and where the visitor got in.

→ Put an X in the box next to the sentences that answer the question.

1. What had the visitor done?

In the kitchen:

☐ A pan of soup had been spilled and pools of it were on the floor.

☐ The food on the shelves had been thrown on the floor.

☐ A bowl of fruit had been thrown on the floor.

☐ A stool had been overturned.

In the living room:

☐ Dirt marks on the carpet showed the visitor's path.

☐ The pillows on the sofa had been crushed.

☐ The blooms on the lily plant had been eaten.

In Sung's bedroom:

☐ The igloo she made for a school project had been stepped on.

☐ The balloon she was given at a party had been let loose from her bed.

☐ A cartoon on the wall had been removed.

In the bathroom:

☐ Toothpaste had oozed all over one of the shelves.

☐ Some shampoo had been spilled on the bathmat.

☐ The mirror on the wall had been broken.

2. The visitor got in by

☐ a tunnel leading into the house

☐ an open window

☐ a hole in the roof

3. Who was the visitor?

☐ a burglar

☐ a baboon who had escaped from the zoo

☐ a raccoon

A final clue: If you peer closely at the picture you will see that the visitor is happily snoozing in one of the rooms!

✎ Write about the raccoon's adventure in Sung Soo's home as if you were the raccoon. Tell about the things you see and the fun that you are having.

Baboon Troop

Read the passage and see if you can figure out the meaning of the words in bold print.

Learn to read this word: **through**

How do you think baboons show that they are fond of each other?

     (a) hugging and kissing like humans
     (b) running their fingers through each other's hair
     (c) pulling each other's tails

    Dusk falls and the moon begins to shine on the grasslands in Africa. Groups of baboons quietly gather before going to sleep. They sit close together, running their fingers **through** each other's hair. Baboons **groom** each other often. It helps them keep clean, and it's their way of showing fondness for each other.

    Baboons rely on each other a lot. They have to protect each other. On the grasslands where they spend much of their time, there are no trees nearby where they can escape from their enemies.

Source: National Geographic *World,* June 1981.

Baboons live together in **troops** of different sizes. The usual **troop** has forty or so members. The **troop** members eat, sleep, play, and travel together. Females stay with the same **troop** for life. Many males leave their **troop** and go to another one when they become adults. Some move often from **troop** to **troop**.

Baboons have many enemies, such as wild dogs, hyenas (hy-e-nas), lions, leopards, and humans who hunt and shoot them.

The males defend the **troop**. They are much bigger than the females. They probably weigh (way) just as much as you do. They have sharp eyes that help them spot enemies from far away. And they have sharp teeth for attacking them.

Baboons may travel a long way for their food. In the dry season they may have to go several miles a day to find food They eat insects, berries, roots, plants, tender grass, and sometimes animals that are not very big.

When baboons are traveling, they always keep the same order in the **troop**. The females and children stick closely to the strongest males. The other males travel at both ends to watch for enemies. If the **troop** meets an enemy, the males band together while the females flee with their children.

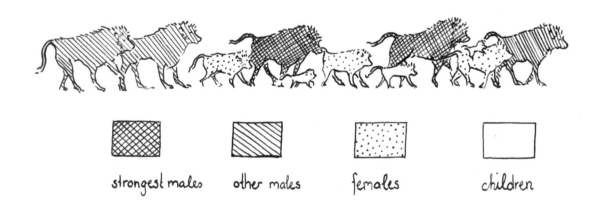

strongest males   other males   females   children

→ Reread the passage and then circle the correct answer.

1. Baboons show they are fond of each other by
   (a) hugging and kissing like humans
   (b) running their fingers through each other's hair
   (c) pulling each other's tails

2. Groom means   (a) to hurt   (b) to make neat, to clean

3. Troop means   (a) a group   (b) being alone

4. Members of a baboon troop
   (a) do everything together
   (b) only travel together

5. Baboons have a hard time feeding themselves in
   (a) the wet season
   (b) the dry season

6. Baboons try to defend themselves from enemies by
   (a) hiding in trees
   (b) banding together

7. The members of the troop who go first and last when
   they travel together are
   (a) the strongest males
   (b) the other males

✎ Describe 6 facts that you have learned about baboons.

Lesson 16: Irregular Double Vowel OO as in Foot

When the vowels **OO** come together, they have an **unexpected sound** as in f**oo**t.

foot

Sound out the letters to read each word.

book	wood	wool	look
good	took	foot	hook
cook	nook	shook	stood
woods	hood	hoof	crook

cookbook	crooked	woolen	brook
good-bye	dogwood	cookies	wooden
rookie	notebook	childhood	woodwind
footpath	goodness	woodpecker	fishhook

Remember these words that have the short **oo** sound:

could   would   should

➔ Choose one of the words from the list to answer each riddle.

1. It's black and white and "read," and you can find it in a library: _____

2. If you like something you say it is: _____

3. What a tree is made of: _____

4. It's the same as a stream:

_____

5. It comes from sheep and is warm: _____

6. You blow into this musical instrument.

_____

7. It pecks on trees looking for insects:

_____

8. You look up ways to make meals in a:

_____

9. You can hang your coat on it, or catch a fish with it:

_____

10. When there are many trees they are called:

_____

11. They make a tasty snack:

_____

12. You stand on this: _____

→ Add **oo** to find the name of each picture. Then write the number of the picture in the box.

☐ w____d

☐ f____t

☐ b____k

☐ c____kies

☐ h____d

☐ br____k

☐ c____k

☐ f____tball

☐ h____k

1.   2.   3.

4.   5.   6.

7.   8.   9.

→ Read each sentence and circle the missing word. Then write the word on the line.

1. They _____ hands and said good-bye.

   took   look   shook

2. Hilary has a warm _____ coat with a hood.

   wooden   woolen   crooked

3. When Mickey pulled the strings of the _____ puppet, it stood up.

   wooden   woolen   woolly

4. "You're a good _____. These cookies are great!" said Wendy.

   book   crook   cook

5. My dog Fido _____ his wet coat after he had been in the brook.

   hook   rook   shook

6. Dad took Carly to the library to get some

   _____.

   cookies   hooks   books

7. The woodpecker was _____ for insects in
   the tree trunk.

   cooking   looking   looked

8. They took the footpath through the _____.

   woolen   wooden   woods

→ Draw a line between the beginning and the end of each
   compound word.

wood	print	drift	bye	man	path
foot	shelf	bare	hook	foot	hood
cook	pile	fish	wood	note	wind
book	book	good	foot	wood	book

→ Read the top statement in bold print. Then put an X in the box next to each sentence that you think is a good reason for the top statement.

1. Woody Woodruff would be a good person to be the captain of the football team.

☐ Woody is a good player.

☐ Woody makes good cookies for the team to eat after the game.

☐ Woody keeps a scrapbook of football stars.

☐ The other team members like Woody and listen to what he says.

2. It was time for Brook to take back her library book.

☐ It was Thursday and the book was due on Friday.

☐ She said it was a good book.

☐ She had finished the book.

☐ The book told of Thomas Jefferson's childhood.

3. The Rooneys needed some more firewood.

☐ The fire was not burning.

☐ Mrs. Rooney had put on the last log from the woodpile.

☐ Mr. Rooney went to the woodshed and it was empty.

☐ They went into the woods and chopped up a tree.

When the **vowels OO come together,** they have **unexpected sound,** as in m**oo**n and f**oo**t.

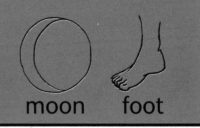

moon   foot

→ Draw a line between the words that rhyme.

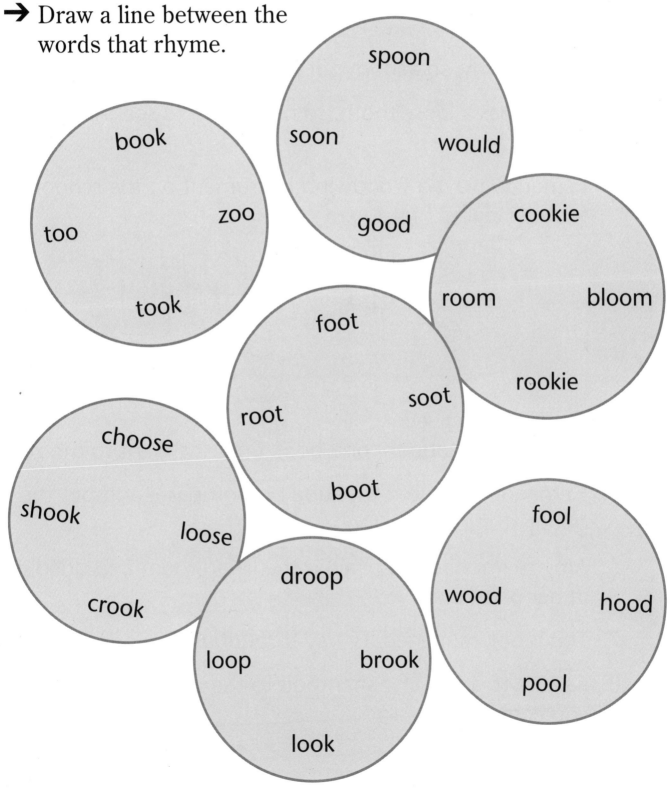

spoon

soon   would

good

book

zoo

too

took

cookie

room   bloom

rookie

foot

root   soot

boot

choose

shook

loose

crook

droop

loop   brook

look

fool

wood   hood

pool

→ Add a letter to make a word.

__ook __oot __ood __oo __oose

coo__ woo__ too__ boo__ shoo__ stoo__

→ Circle the word that does not fit in each sentence.

1. It was sunny, so Sandra put on her waterproof boots.

2. Danny has a loose tooth, so he's going to see the foot doctor.

3. Fernanda plays a woodwind instrument on the school football team.

4. Kay had never seen a kangaroo, a baboon, or a book until she went to the zoo.

5. Hernando squeezed the tube of toothpaste and put the gooey stuff onto his food.

6. Amy shampooed her hair in the living room and dried it in her bedroom.

7. The brook munched its way through the woods.

8. Be sure to add some shampoo to the mushrooms when you cook them.

Hooked on Hooping It Up!

 Read the passage. Then write in the answer to this question:

What game began with two fruit baskets and became a favorite American sport? _____

Learn to read this word that has the **oo** sound as in moon:
fruit

I bet you've spent a good deal of time playing or watching basketball. But did you know that the game started with two **fruit** baskets?

In 1890, Dr. James Naismith was asked by his boss at the YMCA to come up with a game that could be played inside in the winter. He made up the rules for a game with two teams, a ball, and a goal at each end of a big room. On the day of the first game, a janitor nailed up a **fruit** basket at each end of the room. And soon the players were scrambling to put the ball into the baskets.

In time the basket has become a metal hoop with a net made of cord. The rules have been altered to speed up the game and increase the score. But the object of the game has stayed the same—to shoot the ball into the basket and to score more baskets than the other team.

Source: National Geographic *World*, Feb. 1983.

➜ Write in the missing letters to complete the **oo** words in each sentence. Then reread the sentences to learn more basketball facts and tips.

1. To shoo___ well, keep the ball evenly between your hands, using your fingers and the top part of your palms.

2. When ___ ___ ooting, extend your ___ ___ooting hand straight up to the basket so the ball won't be crook ___ ___.

3. If you loo___ the ball up, it will drop into the basket.

4. To be a ___ood dribbler, keep your body low and use just your fingers, not all of your hand.

5. Loo___ up when you dribble so that you can see if a teammate is free.

6. Keep a noteboo___ of goo___ plays to try.

7. A ___ookie is a first-year member of a team.

8. A basketball is a different shape from a ___ootball.

9. If you are like a lot of Americans, you are ___ooked on basketball!

✎ Basketball is a popular sport. Tell about your favorite sport and why you like it.

The King Who Burned the Cakes

📘 Read the story.

If you went to school in England, you would know this story of King Alfred and the cakes.

What was a king doing cooking cakes?

What is the lesson of the story?

Many, many years ago—in fact, way back in the 870s!—King Alfred ruled England. He was good and wise, and ruled fairly. But while he was king, the Vikings rose up against him. They were fearless pirates who had invaded England and made their home on the east coast.

The Vikings were too strong for Alfred and his men and they soon defeated them. They took many of the English as prisoners, but Alfred escaped.

Alfred was badly hurt, with a deep cut in his arm. He dressed himself in a cloak with a hood so that he would look like a shepherd and the Vikings would not catch him.

For several days he made his way through marshlands. Then late one afternoon, he came to a wooded island. He crossed the brook onto the island and followed a footpath through the woods. Finally he came to a woodcutter's small hut.

The roof had a hole in it, and the woodwork needed repair. The woodcutter was very poor.

Alfred was weak from lack of food, and he was in pain from the cut in his arm. He leaned against the side of the hut, too tired to go any further.

The woodcutter's wife came to see who was there.

"Yes?" she said, looking at the drooping man in the dirty cloak and muddy boots. "What do you want?"

"Good lady, I am tired and hungry. Could you spare me some food and let me rest for a while?"

The woman took pity on Alfred and took him into her hut. She said, "We do not have much food. But you may come in and share what we have."

➔ Checking up: see if you are following the story. Circle the correct answer.

1. Alfred ruled England in the 1800s. (a) yes (b) no

2. The Vikings had invaded England. (a) yes (b) no

3. Alfred had a bad cut on his leg. (a) yes (b) no

4. Alfred came to an island. (a) yes (b) no

5. Alfred was so tired that he could go no further than the hut. (a) yes (b) no

6. The woman refused to give food to Alfred.

   (a) yes (b) no

The woman helped Alfred take off his cloak and boots, and she bathed his arm. Then she pulled a stool next to the fire and said, "You can get yourself warm and do me a favor at the same time. I have to feed the animals. Will you look after these cakes that I'm cooking? They're all we have for supper, so be sure you don't let them burn."

Alfred said that he would watch the cakes carefully. But he was soon thinking of the best way to defeat the Vikings. When the woodcutter's wife returned, the cakes were burned to ashes.

"You fool! You fool!" she cried as she shook her fist at him. "Look what you've done. You have ruined the supper and we have no other food left." She continued to call Alfred a fool for several minutes. Then her husband came home.

He listened to what she said but then he recognized that this man was King Alfred.

"Hush, hush, dear!" he said. "Look at who you are speaking to. It is the king."

"Oh no! Oh my goodness!" his wife gasped, and she flung herself at Alfred's feet, begging him to forgive her.

Alfred, who had remained silent all this time, took her hands in his and pulled her to her feet.

"You are a good woman," he said. "You took me into your home and looked after me. I am the one who should ask to be forgiven. I took on the job of looking after the cakes and I let them burn. When you take on a job, it is your duty to see that you do it well."

The woodcutter, his wife, and Alfred went to bed with no supper. When Alfred woke up the next day, he felt rested and he went on his way.

Alfred soon gathered his men together again and defeated the Vikings. And to this day you can see the shape of a big white horse that they carved into a hillside to mark the victory.

➜ Circle the correct answer.

1. Alfred dressed up as a (a) shepherd   (b) woodcutter

2. Alfred wanted to
    (a) find the Vikings
    (b) escape from the Vikings

3. He burned the cakes when
    (a) he fell asleep
    (b) he was thinking of other things

4. Alfred said he would
    (a) not forgive the woman for calling him a fool
    (b) forgive the woman, for she was good, and he was
        the one who should be blamed

5. In the end, Alfred (a) defeated the Vikings
    (b) did not defeat the Vikings

✎ Alfred made a mistake when he burned the cakes. Write about a mistake that you made and tell what happened.

Lesson 18: Irregular Double Vowels OI and OY

When the **vowels OI** and **OY come together,** they have an **unexpected sound** as in boil and boy.

boil   boy

Sound out the letters to read each word.

toy	soil	joy	join
oil	coy	coin	foil
noise	toil	coil	point
spoil	joint	Roy	moist

broil	loyal	enjoy	avoid
poison	destroy	hoist	employ
pointed	joyful	royal	noisy
soybean	appointment	annoy	ointment

➜ Match the words with their meanings.

_____ 1. moist   (a) wet, damp
_____ 2. spoil   (b) to ruin, to go bad
_____ 3. joint   (c) where two parts, like bones, meet

_____ 1. destroy   (a) to bother, pester
_____ 2. royal   (b) kingly
_____ 3. annoy   (c) to do away with

_____ 1. toil   (a) to work hard
_____ 2. coil   (b) faithful
_____ 3. loyal   (c) to wind in rings

_____ 1. avoid   (a) to hire
_____ 2. employ   (b) to keep away from
_____ 3. jointly   (c) together

➔ Circle the name of the picture.

foil boil broil spoil	oily oyster ointment appointment
join joint point pencil	toil tool soot soil
loyal royal moist hoist	coy coin coil cool
enjoy employ annoy destroy	nose noise noon nook

→ Choose a word from the list to complete each sentence.
Then write the word on the line.

1. To avoid spraying poison on his plants, Mr.
   Royal looked up other ways to get rid of
   the insects that were _____ them.

   avoid

2. Dogs are such _____ pets that
   you can always rely on them.

   loyal

3. Mom swerved the car to _____
   the bump in the road.

   annoyed

4. Ms. Royston was trying to take a nap and
   was _____ that the Troy children
   were so noisy.

   destroying

5. Dad carefully _____ up the hose
   after watering the plants.

   employed

6. Mr. Poindexter gets sore _____
   when it's moist outside.

   joints

7. Lloyd was _____ when he was
   asked to join the basketball team.

   coiled

8. Terry was _____ as a cook before
   he became the McCoy's babysitter.

   overjoyed

→ Circle the correct answer.

1. You need soil to grow plants.  (a) yes (b) no

2. Roy is the name of a boy. (a) yes (b) no

3. An arrow has a sharp point.  (a) yes (b) no

4. You can cook a hamburger by boiling it. (a) yes (b) no

5. A dollar bill is a coin. (a) yes (b) no

6. Ointment adds flavor to broiled hot dogs. (a) yes (b) no

7. A gas stove needs oil to make it work. (a) yes (b) no

8. An oyster's home is a shell.  (a) yes (b) no

9. Poison ivy is a good plant to grow in the garden. (a) yes (b) no

10. You should avoid anything marked "Poison." (a) yes (b) no

11. A hippopotamus enjoys being in the water. (a) yes (b) no

12. You will destroy a tree if you strip off its bark. (a) yes (b) no

Roy Robin

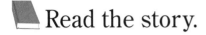 Read the story.

Learn to read this word: **worm**
Remember the sound of this word: **work**
Use these two words to fill in the lines.

Roy Robin was overjoyed. It had rained. The soil would be beautifully moist so he could dig for _____s.

He left his nest and made his way to Mr. Boyd's garden. He enjoyed going there, for he could always find plenty of _____s and other good things to eat.

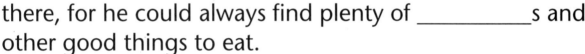

As he got near, he spotted Mr. Boyd wearing a T-shirt and his corduroy gardening pants. He was planting poinsettias. The two Boyd boys were noisily playing with their toys. And Floyd, their dog, was digging in the soil. Through the window Roy Robin could see Mrs. Boyd. She looked annoyed, for she had just spoiled the pork chops she was broiling.

Roy perched on the point of a stick holding up one of the poinsettias. He was annoyed to see that Mr. Boyd had put strips of tinfoil over the grass seeds he had just planted. Roy always avoided tinfoil. It was so shiny that it scared him.

Soon Mrs. Boyd tapped on the window. She pointed to the boys and Mr. Boyd sent them inside to join their mother. Then he went in, too.

At last it was quiet. Even Floyd was enjoying a nap.

Roy quietly left his perch. He landed on the soil where Mr. Boyd had been _____ing.

Was he glad he had come! For there, in the moist, freshly dug soil were plenty of _____s. Some were coiled up in the sun, some were wriggling, some were squirming, but all were perfect for eating.

What a feast Roy had! He was so full he could hardly fly!

"I can't remember when I've enjoyed a meal so much," he said.

Just then Croydon, the Boyd's cat, came along. She had been watching Roy and she was licking her lips, thinking of her favorite meal, too!

Without making any noise, Croydon made her way toward Roy and…

➔ What happened next? Circle the ending that you think is best.

(a) Before long, Croydon was enjoying one of the best meals she had ever had.

(b) Roy spotted Croydon just in time and quickly got away.

➔ Reread the story to find the **oi** and **oy** words.

The number of **oi** and **oy** words in the story is: _____

✎ Write a story about Croydon, the Boyds' cat.

What Is Soil?

 Read the passage.

Which of the following do you think has the greatest value?
(a) gold   (b) silver   (c) diamonds   (d) soil

Learn to read this word: **paragraph**

Wherever you are, you'll find soil somewhere nearby. This is just as well, for we all need soil, and the water it holds, to survive.

Everything we eat comes from the soil. Tomatoes, string beans, salad, wheat, and corn all grow in the soil. Chickens, pigs, and all the other animals that we eat also depend on soil and water. And so do the foods that we get from these animals, such as eggs, milk, butter, and cheese.

But what is soil? Soil contains water and air and is made up of two kinds of materials: (1) materials from rocks, and (2) materials from living things, like plants and animals.

In time, the materials from living things decay and form what is called "humus." Humus becomes part of the soil.

→ Circle the correct answer.

1. Paragraph 1 tells you that
   (a) soil is dirty   (b) we need soil

2. Paragraph 2 tells you that
   (a) all food comes from soil
   (b) only plants depend on soil

3. Paragraph 3 tells you
   (a) why soil is so useful   (b) what soil is made of

4. Paragraph 4 tells you that
   (a) decaying plants and animals form humus
   (b) why plants decay

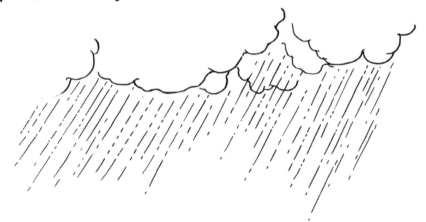

When it rains, water soaks into the soil. If the soil has a lot of humus, it holds the water for a long time. In the woods, the soil has plenty of humus. Leaves, logs, insects, and animals make humus as they decay, mix with the soil, and become part of it.

Deserts are hot and dry. The soil in deserts is usually sandy. There are not as many living things that can decay and make soil in the desert as there are in the woods. There is not as much humus to hold water, so when it rains, water runs through the soil. When it rains hard, the water washes away some of the land.

→ Circle the correct answer.

1. The woods have
   (a) plenty of humus   (b) not much humus

2. The desert has
   (a) plenty of humus   (b) not much humus

3. Which soil holds water for a long time?
   (a) the soil in the woods   (b) the soil in the desert

4. Why does sandy soil not hold water for a long time?
   (a) it has a lot of humus
   (b) it does not have much humus

5. Humus is
   (a) living things that have decayed
   (b) soil with no water

6. A cactus plant does not need much water and would grow best in
   (a) the woods   (b) the desert

All plants need water from the soil. They cannot make food for us to eat unless they have it. Some plants need more water than others. Plants that grow in sandy soil do not need much water. Some kinds of plants can grow even if it rains only one time every year or two. Desert plants usually have long roots that grow deep into the soil. They reach far below to get the water they need. Plants that grow in the woods could not grow in the desert. Their roots would not get the water they need. Plants that grow in sandy desert soil could not grow in the woods, for they would get too much water.

→ Put these sentences in the order they come in the paragraph.

_____ 1. Plants that grow in the woods could not grow in the desert.

_____ 2. All plants need water from the soil.

_____ 3. Plants that grow in sandy desert soil could not grow in the woods.

_____ 4. Plants that grow in sandy soil do not need much water.

✎ The last 2 passages tell you facts about rain and water. Write a description of rain or water that tells what it looks like, such as in a storm or at a peaceful lake.

_____

- -

_____

- -

_____

- -

_____

- -

_____

- -

_____

- -

_____

- -

_____

- -

_____

When the **vowels OU** and **OW come together,** they have an **unexpected sound** as in h**ou**se and fl**ow**er.

house   flower

Sound out the letters to read each word.

out	how	our	now
down	mouse	cloud	clown
loud	owl	south	bow
cow	sour	shout	mouth

round	proud	town	flour
crowd	foul	count	frown
sound	powder	shower	flower
towel	mountain	vowels	thousand

Remember the sound of these words:

your   four   pour   through

➔ Choose a word from the list above to answer each riddle.

1. You put them in a vase: _____

2. The opposite of quiet: _____

3. You use it to dry yourself: _____

4. A lemon is: _____

5. You do this to say 1, 2, 3: _____

6. Where milk comes from: _____

7. Where birds go in the winter: _____

8. You take one to get clean: _____

9. You use it in baking: _____

10. 1,000: _____

11. Actors do this at the end of a show: _____

12. Someone who is funny: _____

13. The opposite of up: _____

14. A globe and a ring are this shape: _____

→ Circle the name of each picture that you see.

crown	cloud	towel	flower
blouse	owl	trowel	cow
mouth	mountain	fountain	brownies
house	mouse	crowd	clown

→ Read each sentence and circle the missing word. Then write the word on the line.

1. I'll need a _____ of flour to make these brownies.

   round   found   pound

2. When Howard got out of the _____ he found that he had no towel.

   tower   shower   south

3. "I can _____ to about a thousand now," bragged Boulus.

   count   amount   about

4. The _____ shouted loudly when the baseball player hit a foul.

   clown   cloud   crowd

5. The brown owl had a _____ in her mouth.

   house   mouse   louse

6. The _____ are a, e, i, o, u, and sometimes y and w.

   towels   howels   vowels

7. _____ house is just outside of town.

   owl   our   out

8. The round candy was so _____ that Camara had to take it out of her mouth.

   flour   dour   sour

How About That!

→ Put an X in the box next to the sentence that answers the question.

1. How were the first wheels made?

☐ The wheel first appeared five thousand years ago.

☐ Our lives would be very different now without the wheel.

☐ The early wheel makers clamped bits of wood together to form a round shape.

2. How did we break the sound barrier?

☐ The jet plane was more powerful than the older planes that used propellers.

☐ The jet plane gave us the extra power we needed to travel faster than sound.

☐ The first jet plane was made and flown by the Germans in 1939.

3. Why do horses wear shoes?

☐ Two thousand years ago the Romans were the first to put shoes on their horses.

☐ Horses need to wear shoes so that their hooves do not wear down and splinter.

☐ A horse's shoe makes a clattering sound on the street.

4. How are elevators powered today?

☐ In 1857, a New York store installed the first elevator for shoppers. It was steam driven and went up five stories.

☐ In the late 1800s, water pressure (presh-ure) powered elevators.

☐ Today, electric elevators whisk us up skyscrapers that are way up in the clouds.

The Big, Round, Brown Potato

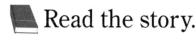 Read the story.

Which do you think has more value—a potato or a cow?
Read the story to find out.

Long ago (in fact, over a thousand years ago), a farmer lived with his wife in a small house near the top of a mountain. It was a hard life going up and down the mountain. But it was even harder farming, for the ground was rocky and not rich like the ground at the bottom of the mountain.

One day when the farmer was plowing, he stopped to wipe his brow, for he was hot. And there, on the ground, he spotted the biggest, roundest potato with the darkest brown skin he had ever seen.

"Where did such a big potato come from?" he asked aloud.

He picked up the big, round, brown potato and hurried to his house. He shouted loudly to his wife, "Lowdeen, Lowdeen, come and see what I've found!"

His wife ran outside. She had flour on her hands from baking. She, too, was **astounded** to see such a big, round, brown potato.

"Why, it must be about two pounds!" she exclaimed.

Her mouth began to water and she said, "What a feast we'll have! Let's eat it now for lunch."

But her husband said, "No, I do not think we should eat it. It is too good for us. I will take it to our king. He should have a potato that is as big, round, and brown as this one."

His wife frowned, but finally she agreed and said, "Yes, you should take it to the king."

The farmer put the potato into a **pouch**, mounted his horse, and went down the mountain. He traveled until he came to the king's summer house just outside of the town.

When he was taken to the king, he bowed low, and then proudly presented him with the big, round, brown potato.

"My, I've never seen such a big, round, brown potato!" exclaimed the king. He thanked the farmer and, seeing his ragged clothes, he took his hand and counted six gold coins into it.

➔ Checking up: see if you have followed the story. Circle the correct answer.

1. The story happened a year or so ago. (a) yes (b) no

2. It was hard to farm on the mountain. (a) yes (b) no

3. The farmer was looking after his cows. (a) yes (b) no

4. The potato was round. (a) yes (b) no

5. His wife had soil on her hands. (a) yes (b) no

6. The king's house was in the town. (a) yes (b) no

7. The farmer was showing his loyalty to the king.
   (a) yes (b) no

The man who farmed the good land at the bottom of the mountain soon heard about how the king had given six gold coins for the big, round, brown potato. He was very rich, but he wanted to be richer.

"Now let me see," he said to himself. "Let me see. What can I take the king?" He frowned as he thought for a while. Then he said, "I know. I'll take that big, fat cow I have. The king will pay me much more for a cow than he paid for a potato."

He took the cow to the king's summer house outside of town.

Like the poor farmer, the man bowed when he was taken to see the king.

"Good, royal king," he said, "this is my biggest and fattest cow. It is a gift to you to show you how much I think of you."

The king looked at the rich man and understood what was on his mind.

"Thank you," the king said politely, "but I do not need a cow."

The rich farmer would not take no for an answer. Finally, the king said, "Very well, I will take your cow. And to show you how much I think of you, I will return your gift with one that cost me four times as much as the value of the cow."

The rich farmer beamed and held out his hand. But to his amazement, the king gave him the big, round, brown potato!

Scowling, the rich farmer left the king's house thinking how foolish he had been.

➜ Answer the following questions.

1. The farmer took the potato to the king
    (a) so that the king would pay him for it
    (b) he felt it was too good for him and his wife to eat

2. The rich farmer took the cow to the king to
    (a) show the king how loyal he was   (b) get richer

3. What did the king think of the rich man?
    (a) The king admired him for being so rich.
    (b) The king could see that he was greedy.

➜ Match the words with their meanings.

_____ 1. pouch   (a) amazed
_____ 2. scowling   (b) frowning
_____ 3. astounded   (c) a bag or sack

✎ Write your own story about finding something unusual or special. What was it, how did you find it, and what did you do with it?

Remember: **ow** also has the **long o sound** as in sn**ow**. This is when it follows the rule: When two vowels come together, the **first one** is **long** and the **second one** is **silent**.

snow

→ Circle the name of the picture.

crow crown	tow town
gown grown	flown flower
row rowdy	stout stow
pillow powder	cloudburst rainbow

➔ Draw a line to the correct ending of each sentence. Circle the **ow** words that have the **long o** sound as in snow. Then underline the **ow** words that have the **ow** sound as in flower.

1. They found an owl's nest   feeding its babies.

2. They spotted a brown sparrow   in the hollow of a tree trunk.

3. From the window they watched the crows   eat from the bowl of grain.

1. The birds have flown south   for summer is coming.

2. The flowers are not yet out   for winter has come.

3. The flowers will soon be the colors of the rainbow   for spring is late.

➔ Draw a line between the words that rhyme.

cow	snow	brown	town	power	pillow
now	crow	blow	low	willow	shower
slow	clown	follow	vowel	glow	powder
down	bow	hollow	towel	chowder	row

➔ Put an X in the box next to the sentence that tells about the picture.

☐ Mandy put the yellow ribbon around the box and tied it in a neat bow.

☐ The clown bowed as the crowd clapped.

☐ The sparrow perched on the branch of a willow tree and watched Mr. Brown sow the grass seeds around the fountain.

☐ Ms. Townsend went outside to feed the sow and her piglets.

☐ Gloria put the yellow flowers in a glass bowl.

☐ Joe mixed the flour and sour milk in a bowl.

☐ "I know this blouse is too big, but I'll grow into it," said Charissa.

☐ "Let's go out after it stops snowing," said Wong.

➔ Now go back and circle all the **ow** words with the **long o** sound. Then underline the **ow** words with the **ow** sound as in flower.

Escape to Freedom

Read the story slowly and carefully, trying to remember the details.

Dowsy was scared. She was tired, hot, and hungry. And she was lost, hopelessly lost.

She had been traveling for seven hours during the night, following the trail from the south. Now, somehow, she had missed the path to the house where she was to stay.

Dowsy peered through the darkness. It was hard to see, for clouds covered the moon and stars. Suddenly, there was a loud sound. She clapped her hand to her mouth to stop herself from shouting out. She quickly crouched down in the shadow of a nearby tree to hide. Her heart beat fast and she shivered with fear. Then she realized it was only the hoot of an owl.

"Wow, you really scared me," she exclaimed to the owl. "I must go on," she said to herself. "I must get to the house before the sun rises or I will be seen. I will be captured and sent back."

She wended her way through the trees, stumbling over tree roots and the uneven ground.

"I can't give up now," she said aloud. "I've been running away for too long to give up now."

Dowsy had been traveling for four nights (nites). She had climbed a mountain. She had crossed a river and nearly drowned. She had waded through a swamp. And she had walked across fields, along roads, and now, through the woods.

At last she came to the outskirts of a town. The husband and wife she had just stayed with had said that she would see a town, and then she would come to two roads crossing one another. And she did! It was a great relief.

She was to go along the northern path. Then she was to count 100 steps. She did this and found a hidden path leading to a brown house with a porch. A white towel with a black cross would be hanging over the rail.

She crept up to the porch. Yes, a white towel was there. Yes, there was the black cross. She was safe!

Quiet as a mouse, she climbed the steps to the door and knocked. A kind-looking woman opened the door.

"Come in, my child," she said, "I have been expecting you. My name is Harriet Tubman. I will help you reach the North."

→ Checking up: see if you have followed the story.

1. Dowsy is traveling at night (nite). (a) yes   (b) no

2. The moon and stars helped her find her way.
   (a) yes   (b) no

3. The hoot of an owl scared Dowsy (a) yes   (b) no

4. Dowsy hid in the hollow of a tree. (a) yes   (b) no

5. Dowsy was traveling alone. (a) yes   (b) no

6. Dowsy nearly drowned crossing a river.
   (a) yes   (b) no

7. She came to the outskirts of a town. (a) yes   (b) no

8. She did not know which of the two crossroads to take.
   (a) yes   (b) no

9. Dowsy found a white towel with a black cross on it.
   (a) yes   (b) no

10. The woman said she was Harriet Tubman.
    (a) yes   (b) no

11. Who do you think Dowsy is? _____

12. Why does she not want to be seen? _____

_____

_____

Who was Dowsy? Dowsy was a slave. A slave is a person who is owned by someone. Her parents were slaves, too. Dowsy did not know her father. He had been taken to another part of the South when they arrived from Africa. Dowsy was a baby then.

What was Dowsy doing traveling through the night, afraid of being seen? She was escaping from being a slave. She was now fourteen.

Dowsy began working when she was six years old. She cleaned the owners' house and looked after their baby. She hated housework. The wife shouted at her, called her "a scoundrel," and often beat her.

Dowsy was sent to the fields when she was eight. Here she looked after and picked row after row of cotton. It was much harder work. But Dowsy liked being outside. She liked to feel the ground under her bare feet. She loved the flowers that sprang up between the cotton. She enjoyed watching the crows flying free in the sky.

One day, as she was watching the crows, she made up her mind that she, too, would be free. From that day on, the idea of escaping was always with her.

When Dowsy was nine, she did escape. But she did not know where to go and she missed her mother. So she went back to her owner, who beat her. Dowsy proudly took his blows. But when she got back to her hut, and her mother put her arms around her, the tears began to flow.

Dowsy's dream of freedom never left her. When her mother became sick and died, Dowsy made up her mind that the time had come to plan her escape. This time, she would be prepared and she would know where she was going.

Dowsy quietly asked around and found there was a way for slaves to escape to the North, where African-Americans were free. It was called the "Underground Railroad." She found out that it did not mean that she would actually go underground or that she would go on a train. The "Underground Railroad" was a secret way of getting to the North without being seen. She would travel at night and stay at "safe houses" along the way. "Safe houses" were houses that were owned by friends (frends) she could trust. Harriet Tubman was one of these friends (frends) of escaping slaves. But she was more than this. She, too, had been a slave and had escaped. But, not content with this, she helped more than 300 slaves escape to freedom. She helped Dowsy to escape far north to Canada.

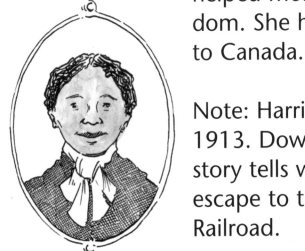

Note: Harriet Tubman lived from 1820 to 1913. Dowsy was not a real person, but her story tells what it might have been like to escape to the North on the Underground Railroad.

→ Circle the correct answer.

1. Dowsy was (a) a slave   (b) a free person

2. Dowsy's father
   (a) died on the trip from Africa
   (b) went to another part of the South

3. Dowsy began working when she was
   (a) 6 years   (b) 8 years

4. Dowsy preferred working
   (a) in the house   (b) in the fields

5. Watching the crows made Dowsy want to
   (a) fly   (b) be free

6. Dowsy's first try to escape failed because
   (a) she ran out of food   (b) she missed her mother

7. The "Underground Railroad" was the name for
   a) a train ride on a subway   (b) a safe escape for slaves

8. Harriet Tubman helped
   (a) 100 slaves to escape   (b) 300 slaves to escape

9. Dowsy escaped to (a) Michigan   (b) Canada

✎ Write your own escape story.

_____

_____

_____

_____

_____

_____

_____

_____

_____

_____

_____

_____

_____

When the **vowels EW come together,** they have an **unexpected sound** as in n**ew**s.

news

Sound out the letters to read each word.

few	new	chew	stew
flew	blew	crew	drew
grew	dew	brew	pew

screw	threw	yew	shrewd
Jewish	jewel	sewer	pewter
slew	mildew	newspaper	strewn

Learn to read these words: knew sew

➡ Circle the words that rhyme with the word in the box.

grew	blew	bloom	dew	cloud	crew
chew	boot	brew	broil	blew	brook
flew	few	food	drew	sew	screw
drew	drown	threw	pew	pool	yew

➔ Use one of the words from the list on the right to answer each riddle. Write the word on the line.

1. You do this to food: _____

2. It tells you something: _____

3. Not many: _____

4. A bench in a church: _____

5. They take care of a boat, plane, or train: _____

6. Where waste goes: _____

pew

sewer

few

crew

newspaper

chew

➔ Read each sentence to understand the meaning of the word in bold print.

1. The children's toys were **strewn** all over the floor.
2. It is **shrewd** to shop at different stores to compare products.
3. They cut down the big old **yew** tree.
4. The **dew** on the grass sparkled like jewels.
5. Lew put tea bags in boiling water to **brew** a pot of tea.
6. The toast was so old that **mildew** had grown on it.
7. There was not room for all the Newtons to sit on one **pew** in church.
8. After the airplane took off, the **crew** served us snacks and then lunch.
9. At one time, dishes, pots, and pans were made of **pewter**.

➜ Match the words with their meanings.

_____ 1. dew   (a) a bench in a church
_____ 2. brew   (b) drops of moisture
_____ 3. pew   (c) to make by soaking or boiling

_____ 1. crew   (a) a kind of tree
_____ 2. yew   (b) a team
_____ 3. shrewd (c) clever, sharp

_____ 1. pewter (a) a whitish growth made by fungus
_____ 2. mildew (b) scattered around
_____ 3. strewn (c) a metal made mainly of tin

➜ Now see if you can use the words above to complete these sentences.

1. Drew _____ed the tea while Hanna served the cookies.

2. John left his clothes _____ on the floor.

3. Stewart put the candy in the _____ dish.

4. The _____ on the grass glistened in the morning sun.

5. The oak trees were cut down to make _____s for the new church.

6. It's _____ to look in the newspaper for the sales before going shopping.

Andrew's Adventure

Look at the cartoons and read what it says about them.

On the boat trip that Andrew Crowley took with his mother, there were only a few crew members: Andrew, his mother, Dr. Crowley, who teaches at the university, and three of her students.

The trip was going to be a great adventure for Andrew! Dr. Crowley and her students were going to a tropical island to study its plants and wildlife.

1. The first few days the wind blew well and they made good progress.

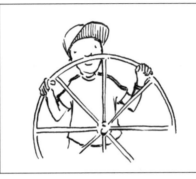

2. The crew got used to their jobs. Andrew helped cook and sometimes he even got to steer the boat.

3. When it was Andrew's turn to cook, he opened a can of stew.

4. On day 6 a bird flew over the sailboat and they knew they were not far from the island.

5. On day 7 the crew landed on the island and went exploring. Andrew and his mother found an immense coconut crab, which they captured and ate for dinner. It was a new treat for Andrew and sure beat his canned stew.

On days 8–14 Dr. Crowley and her students studied the plants and wildlife on the island. Andrew helped each of them in turn—Brewster, Stewart, Drew, and his mother.

6. Andrew cut some stems from the plants, shrubs, and trees that grew on the island so that Brewster could study them more closely.

7. Andrew went searching for lizards with Drew and spotted a 4-foot one! She told him it was called a monitor lizard.

8. Andrew and Stewart studied the colorful flowers that grew in the sandy soil.

9. Andrew and his mother watched the birds as they flew in and out of the trees, and he drew sketches of them.

10. Andrew got a suntan. He felt like he had been on the island all his life. But after 21 days, they had to leave.

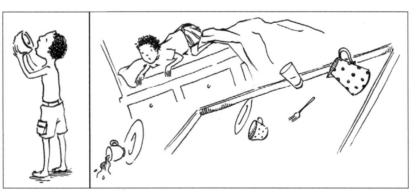

11. On the trip home they sailed into a storm. The wind blew so hard that all the pots, pans, plates, and dishes were strewn all over the cabin. The mainsail ripped and later had to be sewn. But at last they reached home. And before Andrew knew it, he was back in school and the trip to the island seemed like a dream.

➤ Circle the correct answer.

1. Andrew's adventure took him to a tropical island where the climate was   (a) warm   (b) cool

2. Dr. Crowley and the rest of the crew went to the island to study its   (a) volcanoes and rocks   (b) plants and wildlife

3. They knew they were near the island when they spotted
   (a) a bird   (b) a tree

4. Andrew and his mother captured and ate
   (a) a big lizard   (b) a big crab

5. Andrew helped Brewster   (a) look for lizards
   (b) cut down some plants, shrubs, and trees

6. Andrew studied the flowers with (a) Drew   (b) Stewart

7. With his mother, Andrew sketched (a) birds   (b) crabs

8. How long did they spend on the island?
   (a) 12 days   (b) 21 days

9. They ran into a storm (a) on the way to the island
   (b) on the way home from the island

10. After the storm they   (a) sprung a leak
    (b) had to sew the mainsail

➤ Reread the cartoons to make sure you have the correct answers. Then circle all the **ew** words.

What Is a Shrew?

Put an X below the picture that you think is a shrew. Then read the following passage to see if you are correct.

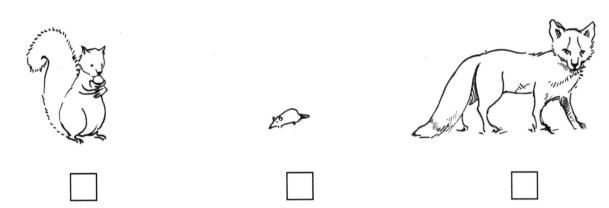

A pygmy shrew looks a bit like a mouse. It has a long, pointed snout, or nose, tiny eyes, and velvety fur. But if you go hunting for one you'll need sharp eyes—and quick ones, too—for the pygmy shrew is very, very tiny. In fact, this mammal is so tiny that it weighs (ways) no more than a dime and could fit into a teaspoon!

The pygmy shrew is usually on the go, darting and dashing about looking for something to eat. It even sleeps in a hurry. It usually sleeps for no more than an hour at a time. Its heart beats at least 800 times a minute, and it breathes 850 times a minute.

The pygmy shrew travels so much that it gets very hot. But its small size helps it get rid of the extra heat quickly.

To get the fuel for all its activity, the pygmy shrew must eat often. It eats its own weight (wait) in tiny animals every day.

If you do spot a pygmy shrew, it's more than likely that it will be dashing after its next meal.

Source: National Geographic *World,* July 1983.

✎ Write a story about a pygmy shrew family as if they were real people who could talk and have adventures.

When the **vowels EA come together**, they sometimes have an **unexpected short e sound** as in bread.

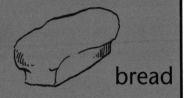

bread

Sound out the letters to read each word.

head	read	deaf	dead
lead	tread	sweat	dread
death	thread	meant	ready
health	breast	heavy	ahead

breath	instead	sweater	leather
heaven	weather	threaten	dreadful
breakfast	measure	wealthy	pleasant
healthy	cleanser	feather	steady

➔ Match the words with their meanings.

_____ 1. lead   (a) to step
_____ 2. tread   (b) not alive
_____ 3. dead   (c) a heavy metal

_____ 1. wealthy   (a) first meal of the day
_____ 2. breakfast   (b) pleasing
_____ 3. pleasant   (c) rich

_____ 1. healthy   (a) made from animal skins
_____ 2. leather   (b) strew, scatter
_____ 3. spread   (c) fit; well, not ill

➜ Circle the name of the picture.

deaf dead lead head	spread bread breath breast
healthy wealthy leather feather	pleasant pleasure measure treasure
read dread tread thread	ready heavy heaven headline
steady instead sweat sweater	weather weapon threaten threadbare

→ Choose a word from the list on the right to complete each sentence.

1. Be careful where you _____. The kids have spread their toys all over the floor.

   feather

2. Henry was sweating from the heat, but he would not take off his _____.

   health

3. It is better for your _____ if you eat a good diet.

   wealthy

4. Pavlo used a tape _____ to see if he could fit the desk in his room.

   deaf

5. Birds' _____s can be many different colors.

   breath

6. Heather was out of _____ from carrying the heavy bags up the steep hill.

   tread

7. "I'd rather be healthy instead of being _____," said Marta.

   sweater

8. My brother is _____ so he can't hear what you are saying.

   measure

→ Circle the correct answer.

1. A deaf person can hear a noise.   (a) yes   (b) no

2. You should use a feather
    to clean your teeth.   (a) yes   (b) no

3. When you are sick in bed you are healthy.   (a) yes   (b) no

4. When you have a lot of money you are
    wealthy.   (a) yes   (b) no

5. You need thread to sew up a rip.   (a) yes   (b) no

6. You need bread to
    make a sandwich.   (a) yes   (b) no

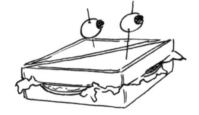

7. You can spread peanut butter on bread.   (a) yes   (b) no

8. You need a sweater
    when it's hot.   (a) yes   (b) no

9. It's easy to lift a heavy load.   (a) yes   (b) no

10. You need a steady hand to throw and
    catch a ball.   (a) yes   (b) no

11. When you're running you can sweat
    a lot.   (a) yes   (b) no

12. If you're ready on time you're late.   (a) yes   (b) no

Wow, I Didn't Know That!

→ Read the paragraph and then write the correct word on the line.

1. A meadow lark is a _____.

A meadow lark is a bird about the size of a robin with brown and buff (tan) upper parts and a yellow breast. It has a sharp bill for catching bugs.

2. The only animals to have feathers are _____.

Birds are warm-blooded. They breathe with lungs. They lay eggs with hard shells. They have wings and nearly all of them can fly. They are unlike any other animals in having feathers covering their bodies.

3. A _____ _____ _____ spins threads of silk that are as strong as steel wire.

Hold your breath, watch where you tread, and protect your head when you get near the web of a golden silk spider! The threads that this spider spins are as strong as steel wire!

The golden silk spider can be found in the southern United States and in the Tropics. The silk thread it spins is one of the strongest natural fibers known.

Islanders in the Tropics weave twisted threads of the spider silk into bags and fishing nets.

The silk would make a long-lasting sweater, but think how heavy and unpleasant it would be to wear!

Searching for Sunken Treasure

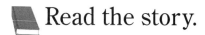 Read the story.

Learn to read these words:
treasure   measure   pleasure   gold

How would you like to find millions of dollars of sunken treasure? Well, the man in this story did! What other treasures did he find?

"Hard work, patience (pa-shents), and some luck," that's Melvin A. Fisher's way of finding sunken treasure deep in the sea. Fisher should know. In 1971, he found the greatest underwater treasure that had ever been found in modern times . The treasure was near a string of small islands called the Florida Keys. They are off the tip of Florida. If all the gold, silver, jewels, and other cargo are ever recovered, the treasure may reach a value of many millions of dollars!

The treasure came from two Spanish sailing ships, the "Santa Margarita" and the "Nuestra Señora de Atocha." The ships left Havana, Cuba, on September 4, 1622, loaded with riches. They were headed for Spain.

Source: National Geographic *World*, March 1983.

Two days after the ships left Havana, a dreadful storm threw them onto a sandbar. Both vessels broke up and sank with all their cargo.

Treasure hunters soon went to work to recover the riches. A few divers found some of the treasure, but the rest of it lay at the bottom of the sea for 350 years.

Then, in 1966, Mr. Fisher began to look for it. Finally, on a sunny day in June 1971, one of his divers found some gold!

Mr. Fisher and his team of divers found coins, gold, silver bars, and jewelry. They also found handmade tools, weapons, navigating equipment to help guide a ship, and cooking and eating utensils. Although these ordinary objects do not glitter, they are treasures, too. They tell historians many things about life in the past.

→ Read these questions carefully, and then go back over the story to find the answers. Write your answers on the lines.

1. Mr. Fisher and his divers found many kinds of treasures. List two treasures that they found that do not glitter.

_____

_____

2. Why are these treasures, too? _____

_____

3. How many ships sank? _____

4. Give the date that the ships sank. _____

5. Where were the ships going? _____

6. Where did Mr. Fisher find the ships? _____

_____

7. What treasure did the first diver find? _____

_____

✎ Write your own treasure hunt story.

_____

- -

_____

_____

- -

_____

_____

- -

_____

_____

- -

_____

_____

- -

_____

_____

- -

_____

_____

- -

_____

leaf

➔ Circle the name of the picture.

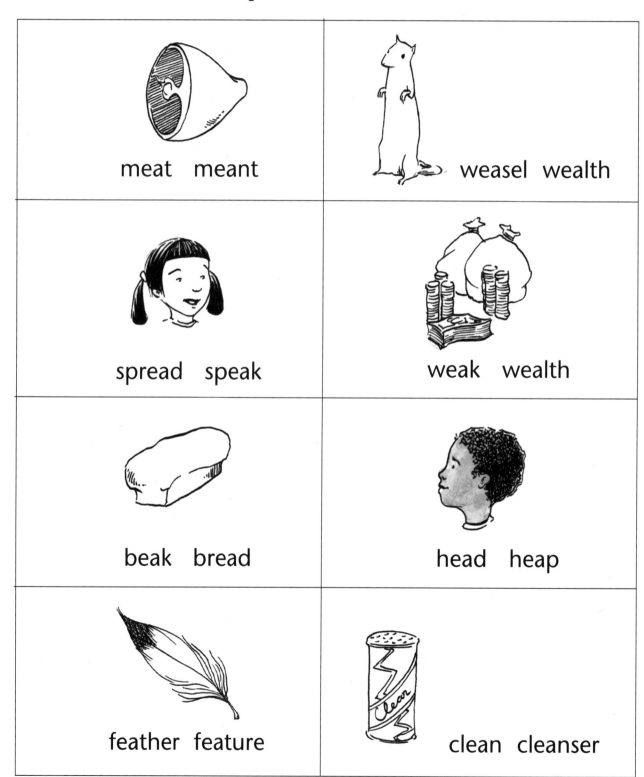

meat   meant

weasel   wealth

spread   speak

weak   wealth

beak   bread

head   heap

feather   feature

clean   cleanser

→ Draw a line to the correct ending of each sentence. Then circle the words with the **long e** sound for **ea**, and underline the words that have the **short e** sound for **ea**.

1. The doll's hair was like   peaches and cream.
2. The color of the rose was like   as a bear.
3. She was as hungry   fine silk thread.

1. Her cheery smile was like   like a leaf.
2. The thunder made the dog shake   a breath of fresh air.
3. The new blanket felt as soft   as cotton.

1. The load was as heavy as   the first snow.
2. The washing was as clean as   leather.
3. The meat was as chewy as   lead.

→ Draw a line between the words that rhyme.

head	team	sneak	health	leather	feather
scream	thread	weak	wealth	lean	mean
season	measure	cream	dream	beast	death
reason	treasure	read	bread	breath	feast

→ Put an X in the box next to the sentence that tells about the picture.

☐ Roy was dead tired from staying up so late reading.

☐ The headlines of a newspaper give the main facts of a story.

☐ "Please don't forget to clean the tub with cleanser after you've had your bath," said Dad.

☐ "This is a real treat," said Estela. "There's no better lunch than fresh bread with plenty of peanut butter spread on it."

☐ Jean says that the reason why she is so healthy is that she eats good foods and jogs three times a week before breakfast.

☐ The reason why Sally does not do well in school is that she dreams a lot instead of studying.

The Elves and the Shoemaker

Read the story. This story tells about some elves who helped a poor shoemaker. As you read, think about which of these sayings sums up the story best.

(a) A stitch in time saves nine.
(b) Too many cooks spoil the broth.
(c) Those who help others will be helped.

"Not a mean streak in him."

"Always ready to help you out."

"You couldn't find a pleasanter man."

"A pleasure to know him."

This was what everyone said about Matthew the shoemaker.

Everything they said was true. Matthew was a good man. But he was also very, very poor. It seemed that the harder he worked, the poorer he became. The reason was that he often did not ask for the full payment for the shoes he made. Sometimes he even gave the shoes away if he knew that the person could not afford to pay for them.

One evening, when Matthew was working late, as usual, he discovered a dreadful thing. He had leather to make just one pair of shoes.

"Oh dear! Oh dear!" he exclaimed, staring at the leather.

With a heavy heart he spread out the leather and measured it. Then, with a steady hand, he carefully cut out the leather so that he would be ready to make the shoes the next day.

He had just finished when his wife came in.

"Come along, Matthew," she said. "It's getting late and your meal is ready. You work too hard. It will be the death of you unless you slow down."

"Well, by the looks of it, I may have to slow down," replied Matthew. And he explained that he had come to the last bit of leather.

They cleaned up the shop so that it would be neat and tidy for the next morning. Then they had their meal and went to bed.

The next morning, Matthew got up in good time to finish the shoes. He had a quick breakfast of bread and tea. Then he went into his shop.

But what a surprise he had. The shoes were already made! And quite beautifully made too—every stitch was perfect.

Matthew put the shoes into the shop window and before long a customer came along. The shoes fit him well, and they were so perfectly made that the customer paid more than usual for them.

With the money, Matthew got leather to make two pairs of shoes. That evening he measured and cut out the leather so that he would be ready to make the shoes the next morning.

Again, he got up in good time to finish the shoes. And, again, he found that the shoes were already made—and as perfectly as the first pair.

A customer came along and paid Matthew more money than usual, so that he could now get more leather to make four pairs of shoes. He measured and cut out the shoes and the next morning all four pairs were perfectly made. And so it went on. No matter how many shoes Matthew cut out in the evening, they were finished by the next morning. So before long he was earning a steady income.

→ Checking up: see if you have followed the story. Circle the correct answer.

1. Matthew was a pleasant person. (a) yes (b) no

2. Matthew worked long hours. (a) yes (b) no

3. Matthew was running out of thread. (a) yes (b) no

4. Matthew found two pairs of shoes the first time.
    (a) yes (b) no

5. The shoes were perfectly made. (a) yes (b) no

6. Matthew always cut out the leather for the shoes so they would be ready for the next day. (a) yes (b) no

Finally, one day, Matthew said to his wife, "Let's sit up and see who is doing this for us."

So, instead of going to bed, they hid in a dark corner of the shop and waited.

As the clock struck twelve, two tiny men, with healthy red cheeks, gleaming eyes, and pointed noses, sneaked down the chimney. They wore ragged, threadbare sweaters and pants, and were barefoot.

Quickly they seated themselves at Matthew's bench and started to make the shoes.

Stitch, hammer, stitch, hammer. The thread went in and out so fast that Matthew could barely see it.

They worked steadily until all of the shoes were finished. Then they crept back up the chimney. "Well, I never!" exclaimed Matthew.

His wife said, "Did you see how threadbare their clothes were, and they didn't even have any shoes? They have made us wealthy. The least we can do is to make them some clothes."

"And some shoes," said Matthew.

The next day, they began sewing. By evening Matthew had the shoes ready, and his wife had made two sweaters with matching caps and socks, and two pairs of thick, warm, wool pants.

Then, instead of leaving the cut-out leather, they put the new clothes on Matthew's bench.

At twelve o'clock, the two elves appeared. And how overjoyed they were when they beheld the beautiful clothes! They immediately put them on. When they found that the clothes fit perfectly, they hugged one another.

Then the two tiny creatures disappeared up the chimney, never to return.

But they had given Matthew a new start, and from then on all went well for him and his wife.

→ Circle the saying that best sums up the story.

(a) A stitch in time saves nine.

(b) Too many cooks spoil the broth.

(c) Those who help others will be helped.

→ Circle the correct answer.

1. Matthew and his wife hid in the shop
   (a) behind a curtain   (b) in a corner

2. Two tiny men appeared at
   (a) nine o'clock   (b) twelve o'clock

3. The men worked (a) steadily   (b) with many rests

4. The men's clothes
   (a) were colorful   (b) had been worn many times

5. Matthew and his wife made each man
   (a) a sweater, a cap, socks, pants, and shoes
   (b) a jacket, a hat, socks, shorts, and slippers

6. The two men came back
   (a) in the daytime   (b) they never came back

7. With "a heavy heart" means
   (a) Matthew was sad and upset
   (b) Matthew's heart weighs (ways) a lot

✎ Tell your own story in which someone helps someone else.

When the vowels **AU and AW**
come together, they have an
unexpected sound
as in **au**to and p**aw**.

auto

paw

Sound out the letters to read each word.

saw	jaw	raw	haul
yawn	cause	claw	thaw
law	lawn	pause	dawn
crawl	fault	straw	bawl

sprawl	scrawl	shawl	haunt
awful	drawer	because	auto
applause	awkward	author	August
coleslaw	laundry	dinosaur	haunch

Learn to read this word: gnaw

➔ Circle the words that have the same double vowel sound as
the one in the box.

yawn	lawn	loud	paw	point	August
cause	coil	crawl	awful	hawk	hook
haul	house	haunch	fault	foot	thaw
draw	saw	soil	because	about	awkward
awful	author	dawn	dead	applause	moon

→ Read the sentences to understand the words in bold print.

1. Paul was **sprawled** on the lawn taking a nap.

2. The **author scrawled** her name in the book she had written.

3. They got up at dawn to watch the **launch** of the rocket.

4. "It's not the baby's **fault** that she is **bawling**. It's because she is hungry," said Claude.

5. Paula put the frozen strawberries in a bowl to **thaw**.

6. The dinosaur **paused**. Then it stood up on its **haunches** and clawed the air with its paws.

7. The mouse **awkwardly** held the cheese in its paws and **gnawed** it.

8. An **awning** is pulled down over a window to keep out the sun.

9. Laura put a **shawl** around her shoulders because it was chilly.

10. The alarm made an **awful** noise when it went off.

➔ Now match the words with their meanings.

_____ 1. thaw   (a) to pull, drag

_____ 2. haul   (b) a shade

_____ 3. awning   (c) to melt

_____ 1. pause   (a) to chew

_____ 2. gnaw   (b) back leg

_____ 3. haunch   (c) to rest or stop for a bit

_____ 1. fault   (a) mistake

_____ 2. scrawl   (b) to write carelessly

_____ 3. shawl   (c) a cover for the shoulders

_____ 1. awful   (a) dreadful

_____ 2. awkward   (b) a writer

_____ 3. author   (c) clumsy, unskillful

➜ Add the missing letters to find the name of each picture.
  Then write the number of the picture in the box.

☐ ____aw

☐ aut____

☐ ____ ____ awl

☐ draw____ ____

☐ laundr____

☐ ____inosaur

☐ ____ ____ ____awberries

☐ ____ aw

1.

2.

3.

4.

5.

6.

7.

8.

➜ Read each sentence and circle the missing word. Write the word on the line.

1. A _____ is a baby deer.

   lawn   fawn   spawn

2. Grass that is dried is called _____.

   thaw   straw   scrawl

3. You use your _____ when you chew.

   saws   laws   jaws

4. A baby gets around by _____.

   sprawling   scrawling   crawling

5. A _____ needs to be mowed.

   law   lawn   laws

6. _____ are made to help us live together.

   paws   claws   laws

7. The sun rises at _____.

   fawn   dawn   lawn

8. Something that is uncooked is _____.

   raw   saw   shawl

Because

"Dad, I need some money."

"Mom, I can't clean up my room now."

"I'm sorry Ms. Crawford, I haven't got my homework."

I bet you've said all these things! But you probably didn't get a very good response unless you gave a good *reason* for what you said.

This is where the word "**because**" is useful—because it tells the **reason why** or the **cause of something.**

➜ Draw a line to the reason you could have given if you had said:

1. "Dad, I need some money   because I have to do my homework."

2. "Mom, I can't clean up my room now   because I want a new bike."

3. "I'm sorry Ms. Crawford, I haven't got my homework   because my dog chewed it up."

→ Draw a line to the reason for each statement on the left. Then put an X next to the sentence that tells about the picture.

☐ The actor paused

because Dad stopped her from crawling on the muddy lawn.

☐ The cat stood on his haunches

because he wanted to reach the bowl of fish.

☐ The baby was bawling

because he was waiting for everyone to applaud.

☐ Laura was yawning

because the sun was shining in her eyes.

☐ They wouldn't go into the house

because she was exhausted.

☐ Maud pulled down the awning

because it was said to be haunted.

✎ Give 4 reasons why you did well on a homework assignment or a job you did at home. Begin by saying, "I did well on my homework assignment/job because. . . ."

_____

- -

_____

- -

_____

- -

_____

- -

_____

- -

_____

- -

_____

- -

_____

- -

_____

- -

_____

- -

_____

- -

Because 2

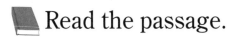 Read the passage.

Did you know that jeans could have been called "Strauses'" instead of "Levi's"? Why is this? Check what you think is the correct answer:

(a) **because** the name of the inventor of jeans was called Levi Strauss

(b) **because** the material used to make jeans came from a town called Strauss

In 1847, a boy in his teens left his home in Germany to start a new life in America. Today, everyone knows his name: Levi Strauss.

Strauss went to California at the time of the Gold Rush. It was called the Gold Rush because many Americans were rushing west looking for gold. Strauss took with him rolls of canvas to sell to the miners for tents and wagon covers. But Strauss discovered that the miners needed sturdy trousers, not tents and wagon covers. He began sewing trousers from his canvas and soon all the miners wanted those "pants of Levi's."

Later, Strauss switched from using canvas to strong, but softer, denim. The pants got their name "jeans" from the name of an Italian town called Genoa (Jen-o-a) where the denim fabric was made.

Source: *Small Inventions That Make a Big Difference. Books for Explorers.* National Geographic Society, 1984.

➔ Put an X in the box next to the sentence that gives the correct reason.

1. Strawberries are called "straw" berries **because**

   ☐ the seeds of a strawberry are on its skin

   ☐ strawberries are often covered with straw while they are growing

2. We stopped using the horse and buggy **because**

   ☐ the horses refused to pull the buggies

   ☐ the auto was invented

3. Spiders do not get caught in their own webs **because**

   ☐ they know which threads are sticky and which are not

   ☐ they weave a beautiful pattern with their threads

4. In the United States, we can see marsupials only in zoos **because**

   ☐ like kangaroos, marsupials are animals that have pouches

   ☐ all marsupials, except the opossum, are living in Australia

➔ Now go back over the page and find all the **aw** and **au** words. Then write the number on the line: _____

Laura and the Dinosaur

As you read about Laura, note the order in which things happen in the story.

Laura lived in the mountains of Austria. She was the daughter of farmers.

One day last August she woke up at dawn. She knew it was the day that her mother needed her to help with the laundry. But it was such a beautiful day that she felt she had to be outside. So the naughty girl put on her shawl and crept from the house.

It was the sort of day that made you want to turn somersaults, and Laura did quite a few as she went along. She watched the hawks fly overhead. She saw an army of ants hauling a straw. She picked some late wild strawberries.

She saw a furry caterpillar crawl across the path. There was so much to see, and she was having so much fun that she did not realize how far she had gotten from her home.

She looked around and knew she was lost. She went on, but she became so exhausted that she sprawled on some straw that was drying in a meadow. After a few yawns, she fell asleep.

When Laura awoke, she saw an immense, awful creature towering over her. It stood on its haunches clawing the air with its paws. Its vast jaws were wide open.

Laura shook with fear. This was not surprising because she was staring at a dinosaur. Yes, a dinosaur!

➜ Checking up: see if you are following the story.

1. This story happened a long time ago.   (a) yes   (b) no

2. Laura was meant to be doing the laundry. (a) yes   (b) no

3. It was a rainy, wet day.   (a) yes   (b) no

4. Laura watched the hawks in the sky.   (a) yes   (b) no

5. Laura saw a snake crawl across the path.   (a) yes   (b) no

6. Laura went to sleep under a tree.   (a) yes   (b) no

7. She saw an awful creature.   (a) yes   (b) no

8. The creature was a lion.   (a) yes   (b) no

"Hi!" the dinosaur said in a pleasant drawl. "My name is Dawn. What is your name?"

"L-L-Laura," stammered Laura. She was awestruck because she had not met a speaking dinosaur before. In fact, she had not met any dinosaur before.

"Laura! That's a beautiful name," the dinosaur said. "I'm glad you have come because I am very lonely. I have no one to play with."

"I didn't know there were any dinosaurs left," said Laura, beginning to feel less afraid. "Aren't you dinosaurs meant to be extinct?"

"Yes, that's true. But somehow I got left behind. My egg got frozen in the freeze that killed off the dinosaurs. Then, a long time after the thaw, I hatched. I crawled out of my shell and here I am! But the awful thing is that I am quite alone."

"Poor you," said Laura beginning to like the dinosaur. "How long have you been here?"

"I don't know. I've lost track. I sleep a lot. Do you want to see the home that I've made?"

"Sure," said Laura. The dinosaur sauntered up the mountainside, and Laura followed. Soon they came to an opening. It was a cave. The dinosaur crawled inside and sprawled out on a carpet of straw.

"You see, it is really quite satisfactory. It's not quite what Mom and Dad would have chosen, but it's not bad for modern times. I would be very happy if I just had someone to be with."

Just then, Laura heard a sound. It was a helicopter looking for her.

Now it was Dawn's turn to be afraid. "What is that?" she asked. "That is a very big bird."

"It's not a bird," Laura grinned. "It's a helicopter, and it's come to rescue me."

"Does it mean it's going to take you away? Are you going to leave me alone again?" The dinosaur began to cry. Big tears ran down her cheeks.

"Oh, dear, this is awful," cried Laura. "I want to be rescued, but I don't want to leave you."

She paused. Then she had an idea. She ran outside and waved to the helicopter.

→ What do you think happened next? What was Laura's idea? Reread the story and then write your own ending. But FIRST, put the following sentences in the order that they come in the story.

_____ 1. "Then, a long time after the thaw, I hatched."

_____ 2. Just then, Laura heard a sound.

_____ 3. She saw an army of ants hauling a straw.

_____ 4. "I want to be rescued, but I don't want to leave you."

_____ 5. The naughty girl put on her shawl and crept from the house.

_____ 6. "Hi!" the dinosaur said in a pleasant drawl.

✎ Write your own ending to the story of Laura and the dinosaur.

A word has as many syllables as it has **vowel sounds**.

cloud	1	food	1
break-fast	2	tow-el	2
an-noy-ing	3	di-no-saur	3
Jan-u-ar-y	4	un-for-tu-nate-ly	5

Remember: When two consonants come together, divide the word between the two consonants.

→ Circle the vowels in the word. Decide if the vowels have a sound of their own or if they go together to make one sound. Then divide the word into syllables with a slash mark. Write the number of syllables on the line.

	Syllables		Syllables		Syllables
pow/der	____	few	____	fault	____
shower	____	already	____	slippery	____
choose	____	loud	____	pause	____
chowder	____	heavy	____	shampoo	____
spoil	____	foolish	____	moist	____
suddenly	____	grew	____	brownies	____
dreadful	____	knew	____	threadbare	____
cry	____	flying	____	treasure	____
jewelry	____	laundry	____	noisy	____
somersault	____	cool	____	dinosaur	____
balloon	____	point	____	February	____
mountain	____	raccoon	____	through	____
spread	____	Jewish	____	journey	____
fruit	____	shrewd	____	carefully	____
pewter	____	my	____	ointment	____

➔ Draw a line between the beginning and the end of each word.

thou	y	show	bye	jew	ed
Au	sand	sew	ish	crook	room
read	ed	fool	ing	mush	tain
point	gust	good-	er	moun	el

joy	er	cook	cause	trea	toon
sweat	ful	aw	er	des	en
auth	al	be	book	wood	troy
loy	or	leath	ful	car	sure

→ Read each sentence below and circle each word that has more than one syllable. Decide if the vowels have a sound of their own or if they go together to make one sound. Then divide each word you circled into syllables with slash marks.

1. Efrain felt foolish when he went outside and found that he was wearing his bedroom slippers.

2. Joy took a shower before going out to dinner with Gilmar.

3. "Strawberries are my favorite fruit!" exclaimed Heather.

4. A baby raccoon and her mother came out of the sewer and trotted along the pavement.

5. "When will you be ready? We have to go soon," said Matthew.

6. Doris thinks that autumn is the best season because the weather is so good and you can still play outside.

7. Paul was annoyed because he had forgotten his notebook.

8. Lloyd drew a picture of the beautiful dogwood trees in bloom.

✎Write a story of your own choosing.

A Wolf in Sheep's Clothing

Read the story. Have you heard of the well-known saying, "a wolf in sheep's clothing"? The saying comes from this story. What do you think the saying means?

(a) it does not pay to pretend to be what you are not

(b) if you brag, you won't get what you want

The wolf was **exhausted**. All day long he had been trying to catch a sheep, but he had not had any luck.

"Now I'll have to eat that awful stale stew that was left over from yesterday," he said, feeling **annoyed**.

The next day, the wolf went off again to find a sheep. But again he had no luck because the shepherd and his two boys kept a **steady watch** over the **flock** all day.

Again that evening, the wolf had only stale stew for supper.

It went on like this. Each day the wolf returned **empty-handed**, and soon he had nothing to eat.

At last he said to himself, "This is dreadful! There must be a way I can get a sheep."

Frowning, the wolf put his head in his paws to think. Then he looked up and saw the skin of the last sheep he had eaten, and he had an idea.

"Of course, what a fool I've been!" he cried. And, without pausing, the wolf took the sheep skin and began to cut and sew.

Soon the wolf had made himself a coat with a hood.

The wolf put on the coat and stood on his **haunches** to get a good look at himself in the mirror. He was more than pleased.

"Yes, it's an very good likeness!" he exclaimed proudly.

The wolf snoozed for a few hours. Then he put on the sheepskin coat and left.

The wolf found the wool coat hot and heavy. And, by the time he had followed the footpath through the woods, and waded across the brook to the meadow where the sheep were kept, he was out of breath.

In the darkness the wolf joined the **flock**. The shepherd and the boys did not discover him. So, for several evenings, he had sheep for dinner.

Then, one evening, the shepherd came out of his house. He went over to the meadow searching for a sheep to have for dinner. In the darkness he saw a very big sheep that he thought would be perfect. So, without knowing it, he took hold of the wolf and killed it. The shepherd was surprised when he discovered that the sheep he was going to have for dinner was the wolf, covered in a sheep's skin. His family went without dinner, but they were happy because they had caught the wolf. And they had learned a lesson.

➜ Circle the correct answer.

1. What was the lesson of the story?
   (a) it does not pay to pretend to be what you are not
   (b) if you brag, you won't get what you want

2. The story is about
   (a) a wolf who liked to dress up
   (b) a wolf who wanted to capture sheep

3. The first time that the wolf came home for dinner without a sheep, he ate   (a) stew   (b) soup

4. The sheep were watched by
   (a) a shepherd and his sheep dog
   (b) a shepherd and his two boys

5. The sheep were kept
   (a) on the side of a mountain
   (b) in a meadow

6. The shepherd came to get a sheep for dinner
   (a) early in the morning
   (b) late in the evening

7. The shepherd chose the wolf because
   (a) he was big
   (b) he was nearest to him

8. Number the sentences in the order they come in the story:

   _____ In the darkness the wolf joined the flock.
   _____ The shepherd and his two boys kept a steady watch over the flock all day.
   _____ He looked up and saw the skin of the last sheep he had eaten.
   _____ The shepherd came out of his house.

➜ Reread the story and find these words. Then match the words with their meanings.

exhausted	steady watch	flock
annoyed	empty-handed	haunches

_____ 1. exhausted   (a) a group of sheep
_____ 2. annoyed   (b) very tired
_____ 3. flock   (c) mad, angry

_____ 1. steady watch   (a) having nothing
_____ 2. empty-handed   (b) back legs
_____ 3. haunches   (c) watching all the time

➜ Choose a word from the list above to complete each sentence.

1. Roy went to the store but he soon came back _____-_____ because he took no money.

2. The birds were _____ that the scarecrow was keeping a _____ _____ over the strawberries.

3. The Lawton's dog sat on her _____ and shook hands with her paw.

4. Howard and Jewel saw a _____ of sheep grazing on the side of the mountain and thousands of beautiful flowers.

5. The Crawfords were _____ from their long journey.

The wolf dressed up and pretended to be someone else. If you could be someone else, who would you be? Tell why you would like to be that person.